Henry *Adams* and Brooks *Adams*

THE EDUCATION
OF TWO AMERICAN HISTORIANS

Henry *Adams* and Brooks *Adams*

THE EDUCATION
OF TWO AMERICAN HISTORIANS

by *Timothy Paul Donovan*

Norman : University of Oklahoma Press

The publication of this book has been aided
by a grant from the FORD FOUNDATION.

Library of Congress Catalog Card Number: 61–6500

*Copyright 1961 by the University of Oklahoma Press,
Publishing Division of the University.
Composed and printed at Norman, Oklahoma, U.S.A.,
by the University of Oklahoma Press. First edition.*

to Genie

Preface

THE EVOLUTION OF AMERICAN HISTORIOGRAPHY is one facet
of the nation's intellectual history which has been too often
obscured by events considered more spectacular in other areas.
Indeed, historians themselves have not been as concerned with
the ideas affecting their own profession as might be expected.
It has only been in recent years that there can be noticed a
trend toward introspection and a tendency for American historians to examine their basic premises and values.

This volume, which developed from my long-standing interest in the processes of writing history, is an attempt to illuminate a single aspect of American historiography. Its focus is
the crisis which was precipitated by the search for a truly
scientific history—a history which would contain ascertainable
and predictable laws. And it uses the writings of two brothers,
Henry and Brooks Adams, as the best examples of such searches.
It is my contention that the writing of history in America was
drastically altered as a result of the Adamses' influence in both
negative and positive terms. In a sense it might be said that a
corner was turned in 1900 which prepared the way for the
advance of relativistic historical thought—an advance which
might not have come so quickly had it not been for the last

great efforts of Henry and Brooks Adams to justify the determinism of the nineteenth century.

This book does not pretend to be, however, either a complete study of the Adamses themselves or of the writing of history. That has been done far better elsewhere. Nor is the claim advanced that it is startlingly original in the material which was employed. What has been made, it is hoped, is a presentation of the rich thought of the Adamses, insofar as it bears upon the search for scientific certitude in history which each man conducted in his own way. Certainly Henry and Brooks Adams invite comparison quite apart from their fraternal relationship.

I am indebted to Professor Bert James Loewenberg of Sarah Lawrence College, who by correspondence and interview directed my attention to the Adams brothers. A very special debt is owed Professor John S. Ezell of the University of Oklahoma, who first showed me the fascination of intellectual history and whose careful criticism of the manuscript was most helpful. I am also grateful to his colleagues, Professors Donnell M. Owings and Herbert J. Ellison of the Department of History, Professor Cortez A. M. Ewing of the Department of Government, and Dean William E. Livezey, for their fruitful comments and suggestions. Needless to say, however, none but myself is responsible for errors in facts or interpretation. Finally, such a list would be incomplete without recognizing my wife Eugenia Trapp Donovan, whose hours at the typewriter, penetrating criticism, and consistent good humor are appreciated more than she suspects.

TIMOTHY P. DONOVAN

Lubbock, Texas
February 7, 1961

Contents

Illustrations

Henry *Adams* and Brooks *Adams*

THE EDUCATION
OF TWO AMERICAN HISTORIANS

I.

The Adams Family and History

AMERICANS HAD ALWAYS FELT a deep dislike for titled nobility. Such repugnance was a natural posture for a people whose roots could be more often located among the lower stratum of European society and whose harsh environment had accelerated the movement toward egalitarianism. Moreover, there had emerged by the time of the American revolution a stereotype of the English nobleman which, although distorted by prejudice and frontier humor, was, nevertheless, an image generally accepted as accurate by large numbers of Americans. The patriotic fervor attendant to the struggle for political independence only further entrenched in the popular mind the symbol of nobility as something particularly antagonistic to the American program of democracy. Indeed, the feeling was so strong that the founding fathers at Philadelphia in the summer of 1787 felt compelled to include under Section Nine of Article One in the new Constitution a provision expressly forbidding the granting of titles of nobility in the United States. Yet, despite this pronounced atmosphere the new nation did produce families that were aristocratic in the best sense—families which seemed to have a natural aptitude for leadership— families which through the mysterious forces of heredity and environment produced outstanding men in one generation after another. Foremost among them was the Adams family of Massachusetts.

The history of the United States from 1775 to 1900 is tightly interlaced with the evolution of the Adams family itself. The first prominent member of the dynasty, John Adams, had played a leading role in the struggle against the British, and he is of primary importance in the establishment of the conservative political tradition in America. Actually, the two aforementioned accomplishments may well be of more enduring significance than his rather unhappy tenure as the struggling country's second chief executive. His celebrated son John Quincy Adams had a public career remarkably parallel to that of his father, and he, too, made more noteworthy contributions to his native land outside the confines of the White House. As secretary of state in the cabinet of James Monroe he was principally responsible for the acquisition of Florida, the enunciation of the Monroe Doctrine, and the formation of an expansionist spirit in the hearts of his countrymen. Furthermore, like his father, he was faced with the rising tide of democracy personified by Andrew Jackson. And just as John Adams had succumbed to the democratic concepts of Jeffersonianism in the dramatic election contest of 1800, so his son was engulfed by the Jacksonian flood of 1828. Yet John Quincy Adams did not retire to the quiet of private life but returned to public affairs as "Old Man Eloquent" in the House of Representatives, an uncompromising voice of national conscience which neither the din of party turmoil nor formal censure could stifle. No other figure so embodies the transition from the dynamism of the young republic to the stagnation engendered by the slavery question.

The tradition remained alive in the next generation. Charles Francis Adams, the son of the sixth president, was extremely active in both the battle of words that preceded the Civil War

and the diplomatic problems that accompanied the holocaust. He had served in the Congress as a representative from Massachusetts and had been a leader in the abortive Free Soil Party which had functioned briefly in the 1840's as a prelude to the Republican organization of the 1850's. After the opening of hostilities Adams had been sent to the Court of St. James's as American ambassador. It was a part for which he was admirably suited, as the virtue of patience, sound moral thinking, and cautious judgments were decided assets in an England which did little to hide its sympathy for the Confederate cause. It would be no exaggeration to claim that a principal factor in the maintenance of British neutrality was the courageous diplomacy of Charles Francis Adams.

The fourth generation of the Adams family produced the two men around whom this book is centered. Born a decade apart respectively, Henry (1838–1918) and Brooks (1848–1927) Adams made their contributions generally outside the realm of public office. Aside from relatively minor clerical positions in connection with their father's diplomatic activities, neither held important positions in the government. This is not to say, however, that they were unimportant in the formation of public policy. No member of the Adams family was ever that, and since each of them were close friends of men who did occupy high offices, their influence was not inconsiderable. Nevertheless, Henry Adams and Brooks Adams were more important as keen observers and analysts of the American scene. In this they were continuing another facet of the Adams tradition in an age which cared little for self-criticism and less for those few who insisted upon examining the new directions undertaken by the materialistic America which emerged from the sectional struggle. It was an age whose *mores* were alien to the traditions of the Adams family, but, ironically, this in itself was typical of the Adams experience. To be forever set against the popular currents of the time was to be expected. And, as always,

5

this happened not because the family did not feel attachment to America; it was because they loved their country almost too well. It is indeed the cynical person who can read the marvelous correspondence between John Adams and Thomas Jefferson, or the monumental diary of John Quincy Adams, or the public speeches of Charles F. Adams without sensing the deep patriotism imbedded within almost every line. Henry Adams and Brooks Adams reflected in their own ways a profound concern for America and her future. That this concern was often manifested behind a façade of both blunt and subtle satire is unimportant. The four great intellectual traditions of the Adams family found a continued outlet in the writings of Henry and Brooks Adams.

These traditions, when taken together, constitute a body of ideas which have contributed much to the spirit and stature of America. They have not always been popular; in fact they have, more often than not, been rejected and refuted by a nation at times unwilling to indulge in an objective self-study. It is this particular aspect which has most often tended to separate the Adamses from the conventional currents of American thought. Throughout the history of the family runs a profound sense of alienation—a tragic loneliness which could only be sustained because the members of the family felt so strongly that what they were preaching was in the best interests of the country they loved so intensely. Indeed, the key tradition around which the others were clustered was the belief that the democratic experiment of the United States must, at all costs, be a success.

All of the Adamses, to a greater or lesser degree, were historians, and as historians they felt strongly that history afforded practical insight into the nature and problems of contemporary society. Looking into the past, John Adams in his writings had discussed at length the growth and decline of previous societies. The promise of Athens had been wasted by the excesses of an

irrational imperialism, and the Spartan totalitarian state had obliterated the democracy of Pericles. The Roman republic had degenerated from the system of limited self-government to the autocracy of the Empire. Successful republican government was the most easily crushed of all political systems. It could be destroyed from the outside as in the Athenian example, or it could be brought down from inside its own structure as in the Roman illustration. In either case the lesson was clear; constant caution was required, excesses of any sort were to be deplored, and the leadership must be ever vigilant to the dangers which always lay ahead.

John Adams felt that in the United States lay the best hope of making the democratic experiment a success. But the republican cause must not be advanced too rapidly, nor must it defy the laws of human nature or society in the process. To do so would be to invite disaster. The lessons of the French Revolution were fresh in his mind, and the parade to the guillotine did not augur well for the emergence of a stable, yet democratic, France. His great mistrust of the Jeffersonian movement centered on the crucial point that the extension of the control of the government to a broader area of leadership was being done too rapidly. Adams was not undemocratic, as his critics so often asserted. Rather, it was his belief that democracy was only possible when its leadership was enlightened and when full recognition was given to the fact that man was evil as well as good, destructive as well as constructive, and irrational as well as sane. Every succeeding member of the family accepted these theorems. Impelled by this belief, John Quincy Adams opposed the virulent democracy of Andrew Jackson as a prelude to the tyranny of the majority. It was a similar motive which led him to denounce the slaveholders of the South at a time when less direct comment was much more in vogue. To John Quincy Adams the perils to the young republic from Jackson and the South had one thing in common. Both had among their supporters extremists, and extremism, whether it sprang from the right or the left, was inimical to the democratic process. Later when the terrors of civil war had been dissipated and the national administration was in the grasp of the "spoilsmen," another Adams, Charles Francis, would become a leader in the Liberal Republican Crusade of 1872. It was inevitable that an Adams should always strive to redress the balance because both their natural instincts and their historical training had convinced them that balance was the key to successful democratic government. The United States had to walk the razor's edge between order and chaos, if it were to succeed where so many before it had failed.

The writings of Henry and Brooks Adams most certainly reflect the power which this tradition exercised upon their thinking. The very core of their disenchantment was their insistence that the America of the Gilded Age had lost its balance, had plunged recklessly down the road to an undisciplined materialism, and that the essence of democracy was being lost en route. The title which Brooks Adams gave to his brother's essays on the movement of history reveals pointedly his thinking. *The Degradation of the Democratic Dogma* had begun, and neither was hopeful that the decline could be arrested. Thus each generation of Adamses had stated its concern for American democracy. More often than not their voices were solitary ones hardly heard above the crowd. But speak out they did, for each believed that the eventual fate of the entire democratic idea was to be decided amid the mountains, prairies, cities, and farms of America.

Grouped around this central tradition of the Adams family were at least three supporting ideas. These concepts were, in essence, basic devices which the Adamses employed to attain the realization of the major goal. This is not to say that the ideas mentioned below were the only strains of continuity that linked family members from one generation to the next. There were many others but the following were the most crucial. They were: a belief in the rational as opposed to the emotional approach to public issues, a belief in the necessity of an educated leadership, and a belief in the necessity of continual national self-analysis. All, they affirmed, were essential if the democratic experiment in America was to enjoy success.

One of the greatest perils which democracy faced was the ever present tendency in such a society to allow its policy to be dictated by the emotional attitudes of the popular majority rather than by the analytical reasoning of an enlightened leadership. Each Adams felt this very strongly—at times to the point of obsession. It was not accidental, therefore, that the accomplishments of the Adamses were invariably more noteworthy in the field of diplomacy, where public interference was less direct, than in domestic matters, where public pressure reached a maximum of feeling. John Quincy Adams' expert handling of the Florida question and his central role in the formation of the Monroe Doctrine are prime examples. A similar assertion can also be made concerning the diplomatic experience of John Adams and Charles Francis Adams. American democracy, with its constant contending for political victory capped by the presidential candidates' appeal to the voters every four years, was in itself a system which afforded excellent opportunity for the demagogue. No Adams ever underestimated the capacity of human nature for self-delusion or the ability of an unscrupulous politician to sway the judgment of the electorate through emotional devices. The differences between John Adams and Thomas Jefferson, between John Quincy Adams and Andrew Jackson, between Charles Francis Adams and the Republican radicals of the Grant era are certainly in part to be explained by the Adams insistence upon unemotional solutions to problems affecting the national interest. In the works of Henry and Brooks Adams there can be discovered the same intellectual position. The former expressed little confidence in the average

American's ability to govern himself in a world which had been transformed by technology. One of the great tragedies of the modern society to Henry Adams was the fact that at a time in history when the utmost in rationality was demanded, irrationality seemed to be on the increase. It was not a time, he declared, to reaffirm the old simplicities but a time which compelled the untangling of the new complexities. And Brooks Adams' solitary purpose in exploring the movement of history was to implore both the citizen and his government to apply "scientific" principles to the problems of existence. This insistence by the Adamses upon the positive requirements for sanity, balance, and objectivity in public life was a corollary to their faith in the significance of the democratic experiment. Moreover, it marks all of them as true participants in the conservative tradition. It may be true that each, in turn, was out of touch with the popular course of the republic, that each lacked the liberal faith in humanity's goodness. But it is indeed the unthinking person who is not impressed with the John Adams who accepted the most unpopular task of defending in a colonial court the British soldiers accused of murder in the famed Boston Massacre. For Adams the choice was simple enough; justice required the use of reason, not emotion, for he realized that one of the most vicious of tyrannies was that of the popular majority.

Closely allied to the belief in rationalism was the Adams postulate of an educated leadership. There is an obvious relationship between the two propositions, for if public policy is to be pursued on a rational basis, the architects of such policy must perforce be something of an intellectual elite. However, the individual family members were at some variance concerning the nature of the educational process requisite for producing the necessary leaders. Like Edmund Burke, John Adams contended that there existed a natural aristocracy which under normal circumstances would find its way to positions of primacy. In a sense, then, democracy by its internal nature put stumbling blocks in the way of this natural process. The problem, according to Adams, was to remove the obstacles without altering the democratic spirit. Adams was often unjustly accused of being overly sympathetic to the idea of a titled nobility. This was not the case. The aristocracy of which he spoke was based on the natural assumption that men were not created equal when it came to such matters as talent, ability, and intellectual endowment. Moreover, he concluded that because of their natural superiority, such aristocrats would soon be identified and would be given responsibilities commensurate with their talents. His greatest fear was that the elective system of a democratic republic might thwart the process and leave the nation without competent guidance in hours of crisis.

John Quincy Adams also firmly believed in an educated leadership, but he placed his emphasis more on the potentialities of education than did his father. Ironically, the thinking of the younger Adams was more closely related in this area to that of Thomas Jefferson, the great rival of his father in the election campaign of 1800. Indeed, John Quincy Adams was much more the democrat, and he was convinced that education of the proper sort could offset the leveling tendencies inherent in a democracy. It was with this in mind that he proposed as president the establishment of a national university whose purpose would be the training of future American leaders. He was basically the scholar in his approach toward governmental affairs and problems, and he was to discover with sorrow in 1828 that the American body politic has an innate distrust of the intellectual. What was required to compensate for such distrust was nothing less than an education which would enlighten the masses themselves in the hope that his enlightenment would in turn be manifested at the polls.

Both Henry Adams and Brooks Adams concluded that such an educational technique was impossible. The world was moving too rapidly for any but a few to comprehend its direction. *The Education of Henry Adams* was itself the chronicle of one man's attempt to understand the world in which he lived, and its author was to describe the attempt as a failure. What was desperately required, then, was a leadership which could chart a course through the awesome entanglements of modern life. In different ways, Henry and Brooks Adams looked to science for such leaders. Each rejected their great-grandfather's assumption that a natural aristocracy would emerge. The parade of political incompetence that stretched from Hayes through McKinley was shattering proof that no such system operated in *post bellum* America. Each also rejected the hope of their grandfather in a system of education designed to provide a climate of opinion favorable to intellectual leadership. Both maintained that with the world accelerating to a point of maximum crisis in the near future there was no time for such an idealistic program. If America and her democracy were to be preserved, superior leaders had to be found immediately.

Finally, the Adams family maintained that the democratic society must constantly re-examine its purposes and analyze its methods. There is a definite moral undercurrent to this demand which betrays the Puritan environment from which it sprang. The Adamses as a group were greatly concerned with the moral posture of the United States. Nor was this attitude particularly confined to them; it has been throughout our history a national mania. Americans have always felt the compulsion to find moral sanction for their actions. More than most nations the United States has tended to believe that its motives must forever proceed from altruism rather than from national self-interest. To the Adamses this impulse did not have its origins in simple rationalization but in the firm conviction that the fate of democracy was interwoven with the fate of the United States. America had a destiny to fulfill before the world, and its realization was dependent upon the maintenance of good intentions as well as good deeds. This sense of mission has frequently been noted by historians of our culture, and it burned brightly in the thoughts of the Adams family.

The accomplishment of the American mission necessitated a thorough understanding of the past. In this sense all of the Adamses were historians. Perhaps it was the uniqueness of the American experience which made American intellectuals seek some sort of guidepost in history. Perhaps the Puritan heritage with its stress upon the unfolding of God's plan through the historical mechanism was responsible. But whatever the motives, the Adamses believed strongly in the efficacy and utility of historical training. Its study was the device by which the conscience of the nation could be maintained, and each Adams reminded his own generation of the ideals which had served as the foundation of the republic.

Not only did history serve as a moral discipline, but it also acted as a primary agent in the preparation of the country's leaders. Both John and John Quincy Adams were expert at drawing parallels between their own times and those of the past. The record of human experience was practically all upon which man had to rely, and both believed that it was sheer folly to ignore it. Henry and Brooks Adams were, of course, historians in the fullest sense of the word. Yet, they were never antiquarians, and their search for an absolute historical law offers considerable evidence that they studied history for solutions to the most practical of all problems: the future of mankind and the probabilities for success of American democracy.

The Adams family, then, has been intimately associated with both the physical course of American history and its intellectual mainstream. They have consistently stood for a body of traditions which represent their most enduring contribution to the national life. That a family should occupy such a significant place during four generations was unique and remarkable. Such achievement speaks well for the values of family tradition, but it also is indicative of the individual vitality of each member. For it is never enough to possess a rich inheritance; what is equally important is to be able to take advantage of it. The latter is by far the more difficult and the more praiseworthy. Standards of family accomplishment may be obstacles as well as aids. In this context, then, the intellectual achievements of Henry Adams and Brooks Adams are even more remarkable. They became what they were in spite of, as well as because of, the family record. Their heritage was important in their development because they were able to expand upon it and adapt it to their own times. And the times in which they lived were bewildering times, when rapid change in the very nature of human society was the rule. They were times which cried out for someone to give order to chaos. The Adams brothers attempted to meet the challenge by delineating laws for history. In so doing they acted in the best traditions of America's premier family, the Adamses of Massachusetts.

2.

America

and American History

It may be accepted as a truism that the manner in which a people write their history is an accurate reflection of the state of contemporary society and a valuable insight into a nation's mind. The historian, himself, cannot escape from those forces operative in his own time, nor can he ever obtain total objectivity and view with Olympian detachment the story of human consciousness as it develops in the two dimensions of time and space. Both Carl Becker and Charles A. Beard have made this point quite clear in their objections to the validity of a purely scientific history.[1] It is necessary, then, to go beyond the individual when analyzing the writings of any single historian. Not only must his personal inheritance and environment be considered, but also there must be observed those social forces which impinge upon his life and manifest themselves in his approach to historical problems. Nowhere is this any more true than in the cases of Henry and Brooks Adams.

The differences between the America of 1865 and the America of 1910 are so staggering that a description of the changes

[1] C. A. Beard, "Written History As an Act of Faith," *American Historical Review*, Vol. XXXIX (January, 1934), 219–29; Carl Becker, *Everyman His Own Historian.*

which occurred must always fall short of conveying the immensity of the transformation. All historians have been conscious of this overwhelming fact, and all studies of American civilization have been forced to consider the impact which these new forces exercised on the direction of the American mind. Yet, despite historical awareness and concentration, the new America cannot be reduced to a listing of factors which wrought the change. There is not in evidence a single cause and effect relationship which, if memorized schoolboy fashion, can provide the student with the key to understanding. Rather, comprehension is something which must be gained intuitively. It must be felt rather than objectively understood. The complexity of forces is such that no single individual can unwind all of the strands of thought which will lead him safely through this Minoan maze. Never in the history of the world have such radical explosions so altered the traditional, intellectual, and physical landscape in such a brief time; never was man confronted with such totally new concepts and problems; never have historians been so hard pressed to explain what had happened. It was too bewildering. Unable to anchor himself in the outworn dogmas of a never-to-be-resurrected past, often unwilling to push open the doors to a future fraught with further potential for change, and unprepared to meet the challenge of a perilous present, the American floundered, lost his way, and sometimes despaired.

The writer of history shared the dilemma with his countryman. All agreed that the old standards would not suffice; the pleasing criteria of a gentler age were no longer applicable. New formulas had to be discovered, new techniques had to be employed, and a new kind of history had to be written if the story of human development was once more to be made intelligible. Above all the historian was faced with a problem of moral and intellectual reorientation if he was to cope with the energies that had been released. The task appeared to be insuperable. That he did not find truth and an ultimate solution is apparent; that he made the attempt at all is remarkable. The Adams brothers, in distinctly different ways, were two who ventured what heretofore had been considered impossible.

In a very general sense what occurred in the post-Civil War years was the product of the new science which had its roots in fifteenth- and sixteenth-century Europe. There was a direct link between the observations of Copernicus and Kelvin's second law of thermodynamics, between the scientific investigations of Descartes and Gibbs' rule of phase. Moreover, the relation existing between the theories of a Leibnitz or a Newton and the creation of a tremendous industrial complex in America are not as shadowy nor as obscure as might first appear. Advancements in both pure and applied science are closely interrelated. Their philosophical problems often stem from the same source, and it is impossible to separate their effects without warping judgment. The transition from Jeffersonian America to the United States of John D. Rockefeller was a change implicit in Jeffersonianism itself. The unenlightened "robber baron" was as much a product as his machines of the rationale engendered by the age of science. Industrialism, urbanization, mechanization, and immense production of wealth were not thrust upon a nation which had been theoretically unprepared for them. Rather, they made their entrance on the American scene in such a tumultuous fashion and with such rapidity that the theoretical preparation proved inadequate.

It is perhaps well to note specifically what abrupt challenges were brought about by each of the principal new forces in American life. It was by meeting these new demands that the historian shaped his considerations on the meaning of history. At the base of the problem was the activity of science, but such activity manifested itself in at least four unique ways: industrialism, urbanization, technological advance, and theoretical advance. It is easily seen that the four divisions are intimately related; yet their impress on the culture and life of the people was a variable factor, depending upon the status, area of residence, and sensitivity of the individual. The historian of the time was certainly not immune to these restrictions. In each of these areas, then, there are fundamental problems that affected the writing of history because they conditioned the writer himself.

The pattern of industry after the Civil War was not essentially different from what it had been prior to the sectional conflict. The movement toward the large corporation was not unique; it had simply been accentuated by the exigencies of wartime conditions.[2] Certainly, the growth of manufacturing in this country had been proceeding at a steady pace for fifty years. What was different was the greater rate of increase. Men were confronted with the realities of big business all at once. Whereas the ante bellum nation had time to accustom itself to industrial changes, the postwar United States was given no period to make a psychological and economic adjustment. It was another Rip Van Winkle situation, but with a greater sense of urgency and a good deal less humor than that which confronted the Irving folk hero. The simple fact that business and industry were big meant that problems of poverty, labor rights, capital rights, property, and myriad others had to be solved. The whole structure of society had to adjust, and in most instances the adjustment was a violent one. Darwin's notion of the "survival of the fittest" seemed very applicable, for those unable to make a satisfactory transition indeed became but the vestiges of an age departed. Perhaps the most terrifying result was the insistence with which industrialism produced conformity—not only in goods but in men. To the American who had always prided himself on his individuality, the reduction of personality to impersonality was almost incomprehensible. He

[2] This thesis is amply developed in the opening chapter of Samuel P. Hays, *The Response to Industrialism.*

had to ask where he was going and what agencies in his past had forced him down such a cataclysmic road.

Industrialism also meant power—more power than any had ever imagined. How was this power to be used? How was it to be regulated? How were the American image and myth to be kept intact in the face of this power? And as he tried to find answers to these imponderables, the American noted that the rate of power seemed to be increasing in geometric progression, making his vain attempts at solution appear ludicrous and impotent. On every side the American was faced with a bigness he did not comprehend, nor did he understand how to begin his education. This is what Henry Adams meant when he described his own attempt at learning as a failure.[3]

To the historian the force of industrialism meant a re-examination of the past in order to arrive at some explanation of the present. It meant a re-emphasis on economic factors as causative agents in human destiny. He could no longer ignore them in deference to the military, the constitutional, and the political. History had played a huge joke on her own devotees; they had been searching only special areas of the past, and now they had to pay the price of their selectivity. It was either reinterpretation or extinction. Some perished, but others took up the task of telling America what had happened to her and what lay in the future. Brooks Adams saw history in this new light and formed a philosophy on an economic foundation.

Urbanization was similar to industrialism in that it also was a trend which had existed before the Civil War. While the republic had been predominantly agricultural through its first ninety years, there had been a slow movement toward the cities. Again, the concentration of industry and capital occasioned by the sectional conflict had accelerated the movement toward the city. A social dislocation of the first order occurred, and in-

---

[3] Henry Adams, *The Education of Henry Adams*, 53. (Hereafter cited as H. Adams, *Education*.)

stead of the problem's easing after the war, it became more complex. The United States became a nation of cities.

Perhaps the problems created by this rapid urbanization were greater for the sociologist than for the historian, but certainly they were immense enough for the latter. To one accustomed to thinking of this country in terms of a romantic Jeffersonian America, the knowledge that the genteel Republic was forever lost was both tragic and startling. Aside from a personal sense of loss, the historian was now faced with a series of problems for which he had developed no adequate tools. It would not be until well into the twentieth century that history from an urban viewpoint would seem the correct approach.[4] Writers like Henry and Brooks Adams felt a distinct sense of separation from the main currents of their native land. What had happened to the America of more halcyon days? Where was the rugged independence and virility of the small farmer whom Henry had described so vividly in his monumental *History?*[5] Had the nation which produced an Emerson, a Longfellow, and a Thoreau discarded its rural heritage for a melting pot of urban pottage? Many thought so; only Walt Whitman celebrated the birth of a new land and welcomed the city throngs to partake in a democracy at once different and challenging.

The most important problem created by the urban movement for the philosophical historian was one of perspective. Undeniably, any view of history, and particularly American history, had to account for the great cities that were now dotting the countryside; yet there was a danger in pursuing too assiduously the hidden strands of the past for a clue to the present dilemma. The same error of omission might be made.

[4] William Diamond, "On the Dangers of an Urban Interpretation of History" in Eric F. Goldman (ed.), *Historiography and Urbanization: Essays in American History in Honor of W. Stull Holt*, 67.

[5] Henry Adams, *The United States in 1800*. This short volume comprises the first six chapters of Vol. I of Henry Adams, *History of the United States during the First Administration of Thomas Jefferson*.

If concentration was now placed on economic matters to the exclusion of things heretofore considered vital, judgments and prophecies would still be imbalanced. The able historian knew that current pressures must never be allowed to shape entirely a considered evaluation of the past. But the temptation was overwhelming, and some in succumbing decided that what had been written about American history prior to 1890 was useless. Thus, Henry Adams declared his history of the Jefferson and Madison administrations to have been a futile chore, undertaken in ignorance.[6] And Brooks Adams wrote history as if the period of rural America was only a prelude to the urban nation of his own day.[7]

Each denied his spiritual heritage, finding it outworn in what seemed like a materialistic America. Farm and frontier values did not appear to fit into the city scheme. What was ignored by both was the fact that the substructure of American society remained solid. The changes in the physical appearance of the United States had not seriously altered those enduring characteristics which had molded the nation. They were blinded by what they saw and hence lost faith in things true but unseen. Perspective was lost, not only for the historian but for the average citizen who had known a pre-Lincoln America. The Adams brothers, writing in a land they did not know or like, sought solutions to the problems of history in science— Brooks in technology and Henry in theorism. By embarking on a course more uncharted than the one they left and by accepting the certitude of disciplines now known to be uncertain, they arrived at philosophies of history which, despite intuitive insights, suffered from a narrowness that ignored the totality of human history.

Rapid technological advance was another keystone to the ad-

[6] Henry Adams to Raphael Pumpelly, May 19, 1910, in *Letters of Henry Adams (1892–1918)*, ed. by Worthington C. Ford, II, 542. (Hereafter cited as Ford, *Letters*, II.)

[7] Brooks Adams, *America's Economic Supremacy*.

vent of a modern industrial America. Invention and improvement in all the basic industries proceeded at a rate hitherto unknown in Western civilization. The industrial revolution was,
in effect, just that—a revolution. Transportation and communication were completely altered by the invention of telegraph,
telephone, and a thousand other items which shortened distance
and time. Production increased at tremendous rates, and, aided
by countless innovations and manufacturing techniques, a
plethora of goods became available not only to the domestic
consumer but for foreign export as well. The country embraced the technological wonderland as a definite sign that the
American dream of fulfillment was possible in an industrial
age. America was not so much concerned with the scientific
theories which lay behind the new bounty as she was involved
in the trappings of those theories as exhibited in railroads that
spanned a continent, in giant steel furnaces utilizing the Bes-
semer process, or in an instrument which could translate the
human voice into sound waves and then reverse the process to
produce the same voice within seconds hundreds of miles dis-
tant. The old habit of tinkering, of inventiveness, of practicality
reasserted itself in an era when such a habit might easily mean
profit. To the modern technology America most easily adapted
herself, and it was her historical experience which facilitated
the adaptation.

To the historian technological improvement posed two
serious problems. First, what did the alarming increase in
power, both mechanical and financial, imply for the destiny
of mankind? For the answer to this question, Brooks Adams
looked for a parallel in world history. He found not one but
many. As a result of his investigation he gloomily predicted that
America faced a fate similar to Rome's unless power could be
controlled.[8] And second, since the dividing line between the

---

[8] This idea recurs throughout his major work but may be especially noted
in his chapter on the Romans. See Brooks Adams, *The Law of Civilization*

old and new America was so sharply defined, would it ever be possible to view America's youth in any objective sense? Henry Adams thought it impossible. He had lived through the great changes; life would never be the same again. Unlike Charles Beard, he did not envision an emerging utopia which would owe its vast munificence to technological advances.[9] Rather, he saw only chaos; and after having been an orthodox historian for twenty-five years, he turned in the autumnal stage of his life to science as the golden key essential to comprehension. When he opened the door and examined the mysterious contents of physics, biology, and geology, he discerned only additional complexities. Technology made the task of the historian seem imperative. With the world rushing at breakneck speed to a rendezvous with the unknown, some direction was demanded. How could civilization be prevented from perpetrating its own destruction? How much could be expected from a people who could manufacture vast quantities of electrical energy without even understanding electricity? How could the historian hope to wrestle with problems for which he had so little preparation? It was questions like these which Henry Adams asked, and which eventually caused him to despair.

At the base of all the great changes was the new god, modern science, and man surrounded it with as many mysteries and trappings as he had enveloped the nature deities of a more primitive age. If, indeed, the world had cast off the last fetters of medievalism, it still retained a yen for the remote and unknowable. The scientist replaced the priest as the mediator between humanity and the universe; and while his explanations were usually couched in the terminology of mathematics, they were as esoteric to the layman as the Latin incantations of church liturgy. In a sense, also, science proved more dramatic

and Decay: An Essay on History, 9–45. (Hereafter cited as *The Law of Civilization and Decay*.)

[9] C. A. Beard, "Introduction," to J. B. Bury, *The Idea of Progress*, xi.

than religion. It was no longer necessary to depend on second-hand accounts of miracles to demonstrate the power of the Almighty; the miracles of science were in evidence everywhere, from the giant industries to the unparalleled harnessings of power. Moreover, the wonders of science were the handiwork of men. There was comfort in this; it seemed to reduce the vastness of space and time to a knowable quantity. Certainly, one result was to denude God of an anthropomorphic quality, but it also rendered comprehensible to human intelligence what often in the past had appeared beyond understanding. Secularism had its heaven too.

Ironically, science and scientists, despite their protestations to the contrary, yielded to the same temptations as their religious predecessors. They continued the search for a single avenue of truth—one all-embracing formula which could explain man, man's world, and the universe which encompassed them both. The human passion for order and organization impelled the relentless pursuit for the key which would unlock all doors. Just as theologians for centuries had maintained the supremacy of their own particular explanations, so scientists now attempted to interpret the infinitely varied phenomena of nature by unitary theorems which produced as much dispute and intellectual warfare as a sixteenth-century war of religion. Darwin, Kelvin, Gibbs, and countless others saw a scheme to chaos, and each in turn was hailed optimistically as a beacon which would eventually enlighten the world.

What was most important was the impact which science had on the American mind. Rigid patterns of thought were profoundly altered; inflexible ideas that had been originally cast in the stern mold of Puritanism were finally rejected; traditional Yankee values, such as inherent optimism and the serene confidence in native capacities, although not discarded, were now subject to a rigid scrutiny.[10] The nation's intellectuals entered

10 As yet there remains to be written a comprehensive survey of this tran-

on the period of self-examination which was to reach its culmination in the bitter negativism of the literary determinists and finally in the social-consciousness school of the twenties and thirties. The effect of science and the vogue of impersonality which it nurtured were not confined solely to literature, although here they were more dramatic, but they permeated all intellectual areas. It was simply impossible in such an atmosphere to remain unmoved by the new scientific revelations. Art developed the impressionistic school, and the cubists were excellent examples of the scientific influence; religion could either reconcile herself to scientific data or take refuge in a fundamentalism which came to grips with the newly discovered universe by denying it. The social sciences were no exception; the very term "social science" illustrates the force which science exercised on thought. To be heard one had to be scientific. And while the physical and biological scientists were busy providing rational explanations for the world of matter, the social scientists took up the search for laws to explain man and society. Inevitably, history was forced into line; there was no alternative. No greater crisis in American historiography can be found; for if history was to persevere, if it was to become something more than a pastime for romantic antiquarians, it had to meet the challenge flung at it by science.

One element of the crisis which confronted the American historian was the increasing demand that the method of science be applied to the writing of history. Since the term "scientific" had all but become synonymous with truth, the function of the historian was to be as scientific as possible. It did not matter that most historians, even the most romantic,[11] had utilized

sition in American thought. However, the best single analysis is to be found in the introductory chapter of Henry S. Commager, *The American Mind.* Also useful despite its brevity is Stow Persons, *American Minds.* Standard and still illuminating is Merle Curti, *The Growth of Human Thought.*

[11] Joe Patterson Smith, "Francis Parkman," in William T. Hutchinson (ed.), *The Marcus Jernegan Essays in American Historiography,* 49. Parkman,

what was approximate to the critical approach now practiced by the physical scientist. Rules had to be spelled out, and any evidence that the historian was misarranging facts for literary purposes or to support a wobbly thesis was immediately excoriated. The latter part of the nineteenth century witnessed a number of American historians who wrote history with close attention to scientific ground rules. Henry Adams was included in their number. Yet, although the need for historical purity and objectivity was exaggerated, there was a real need for more rational history which could stand on its factual merits rather than on its appeal to patriotism or the aesthetic taste. Nor was such pressure confined only to America; indeed, the activities of the great Germans Leopold von Ranke and Barthold Niebuhr had been the first professional response to a universal demand. The insistence, both within and without the profession, on the employment of the scientific technique had been heard in Europe for two generations before a similar demand was made in America.

The fundamental factor behind the movement for a scientific history was the assertion, derived from the physical and natural sciences, that certitude concerning the past was possible. Just as it was believed that man could penetrate the mysteries of the universe and verify his findings with mathematical precision, so it was maintained that the absolute truth of human history could be discovered through a similar process. Historians had become convinced that a scholarly appraisal of documentary and manuscript sources would deliver as much surety as an analysis of test-tube contents would provide for the chemist. And, in a general sense, this attitude proved salutary to a profession which had long occupied a halfway house between fact and fiction. The writings of Richard Hildreth

---

probably the last of the great romantics, placed great emphasis on the scientific method and the study of documents.

demonstrated both the successes and the failures of the new formula.[12]

Henry Adams and Brooks Adams wrote history according to the scientific method; that is, they employed the research devices which have since become standard in the profession. In fact, some aver that Henry Adams was the first truly scientific historian produced in the United States.[13] Both made extensive use of source material and did not confine their researches to native materials but searched foreign archives as well; both made use of philological, archaeological, and anthropological evidence; and both made a conspicuous effort to escape the eschatological. However, the problem at hand is not the development of the scientific method in American historiography, but rather the involvement of historians with another element of the scientific crisis, namely the drive to uncover a law which might explain the nature and direction of historical phenomena.

The study of history from Herodotus onward had seen numerous attempts to elicit a causal governing mechanism in the historical process. Certainly Livy, Polybius, St. Augustine, Orosius, Bossuet, and others thought that they had laid bare the secret. What was peculiar to the nineteenth century was the belief that only in science could the real law be found. The promulgation and ready absorption of the Darwinian hypothesis was the greatest single factor in accentuating the drive in other fields for similar explanations. In Europe a revival of an eighteenth-century rationalist climate of opinion was soon in evidence. In addition, there was a stronger sense of urgency as the complications of the French Revolution and of a burgeoning industrialism made human society seem more chaotic and incomprehensible. Beginning with the German idealists Kant, Fichte, and Hegel and culminating in the logical positivism of

[12] Michael Kraus, *The Writing of American History*, 130–31.
[13] *Ibid.*, 177; William H. Jordy, *Henry Adams: Scientific Historian*, vii.

Auguste Comte and the scientific socialism of Karl Marx, solutions to the nature of history were offered. Each in his own way based his findings on the record of history, and each sought to show that what had seemed disorder and fortuitous chance was in reality the world-spirit, the movement toward *Recht*, or the class struggle. Of all the Europeans, the great student of Saint-Simon and founder of modern sociology Auguste Comte came the closest to achieving an acceptable synthesis based on the conclusions of science. It was Comte who exercised a major influence on American historians, for his three-stage analysis of history seemed more to fit the American situation.[14] The suggestion of theological, metaphysical, and scientific steps in history can often be noted in Brooks Adams' formulation of a great law, and the implication of inevitability outside human control is readily discernible in Henry's later works.[15]

If the Adams brothers merit an important position in American historiography, their claim to any eminence rests upon their long and determined quest for the law which would make the stream of history intelligible. In the literal sense their search was unsuccessful, but it must be remembered that the environmental context in which they labored was a society which accepted the possibility of scientific certainty in the social sciences as well as the physical and natural sciences. Nor were their attempts entirely unrewarded. For if they did nothing else, they emphasized for historians the positive necessity of arriving at some kind of synthesis as a result of historical

---

[14] This statement cannot, of course, be documented, and many will contend that Marxism was more influential. However, the impact of Karl Marx was on a later generation—a generation which had been conditioned to the principles of economic determinism by the vicissitudes of World War I and the great catastrophe of 1929. Comte's influence was more direct, particularly on the historian who correlated his findings with the avenues of approach suggested by science.

[15] B. Adams, *The Law of Civilization and Decay;* Henry Adams, "The Tendency of American History," in H. Adams, *Degradation of the Democratic Dogma,* 123–33. (Hereafter cited as H. Adams, *Degradation.*)

investigations. Employing the imported German techniques was not enough. It did little good to recapture the past with more precision and clarity than it had ever been caught before, if this was to be the only result. And while it is true that no single pattern probably explains the total fabric of history, it is equally correct that a meaningless history is a useless one. The day of antiquarianism was past. History was forced to justify her existence as a discipline worthy of study and scholarly endeavor. Later, the relativists would attack most vigorously the concept that absolute truth of the past could ever be known. Indirectly, their attack also fell upon men like Henry Adams and Brooks Adams, who had based their conclusions concerning a law partially on the assumption that the past was capable of being discovered in a very real sense. But the relativist ignored the fact that he, himself, made a similar assumption when he claimed that history was only meaningful in so much as it had contemporary validity. For did he not posit the notion that enough of the historical past, distorted as it might be, could be sufficiently knowable to make it a useful tool for the present? Not only does this assumption undergird the relativist position, but there is also implicit in the relativist argument the idea that synthesis and evaluation are required concomitants of history.[16] Thus, it does not appear that those who searched for a meaning to history were entirely engaged in an activity that could never attain fruition.

Henry Adams and his younger brother were both aided and handicapped by their membership in one of America's most prominent families. For a family to have not one but two presidents numbered among its ancestors was unique in American history. And for both John Adams and his son John Quincy Adams to possess such discerning intellects and to have been

---

[16] For the best and most recent examination of the relativist attack on scientific history, see Cushing Strout, *The Pragmatic Revolt in American History: Carl Becker and Charles Beard*.

such articulate spokesmen in public affairs was doubly remarkable. The Adams family was as American as the Massachusetts soil which had nurtured it, and the succession of public figures which the family produced created an image in the American mind which still persists.[17] It is an image largely composed of those virtues which Americans commonly have associated with what they like to believe is the self-reliant man of the New World. Solidity of thinking, sobriety of conduct, and a dignified yet democratic decorum are all components; but perhaps the dominant note is one of faith—faith not only in one's own capacities but also in America and in her destiny. For an Adams to doubt either himself or America was treason to country as well as to family. Neither Henry nor Brooks could ever escape from the image; and especially in the former the failure to elude the public scrutiny resulted in a definite rebellious cast of mind which accented his individuality and, at the same time, jaundiced his perspective. Brooks was also conscious of public expectations and was not insensitive to the remarks that were made concerning his alleged eccentricities.[18] Nevertheless, despite the handicap of never being able to enjoy anonymity, there were concrete advantages in being a member of the Adams family.

One important benefit which accrued from family membership was the access that it gave into the higher councils of society, business, and government. As a child Henry Adams had visited with those prominent in American politics, and this relationship never deteriorated. Brooks, too, was confidant to leading statesmen, as witness his advisory role to Theodore Roosevelt.[19] Ties such as these were extremely important, for

[17] There is no really adequate composite history of the fortunes of the Adams family. The eulogy of James Truslow Adams, *The Adams Family*, is brief and far too sketchy; but it does provide insight into the family tradition and by implication suggests the handicaps which such family prominence can impose upon its descendants.

[18] Brooks Adams, "Introduction," to H. Adams, *Degradation*, 89.

they enabled the Adams brothers to bypass much of the red tape in acquiring source material (particularly in foreign archives) that so often is an obstacle to less fortunate historians. Another advantage was the security afforded by the family's financial status. Although by no means were they among the wealthiest families in America, the Adams treasury was affluent enough to allow its members a certain latitude in choosing their life's work. Nothing is more treasured by the historian than time, and this was a quantity given to Henry and Brooks in abundance.

Yet, possibly more significant than the material benefits aforementioned was the psychological impact which being a member of the Adams family exercised on the minds of the two historians. It was impossible not to be conscious of the heritage which was theirs. Indeed, both were proud of their ancestry, and both felt a remarkably close kinship to their grandfather John Quincy Adams.[20] No man ever possessed a keener historical sense than the sixth president of the United States. No one can peruse his monumental *Diary* without appreciating this fact. Both Henry and Brooks owed an intellectual debt to John Quincy. It was he who interested them in examining with some profundity the drama of America in the story of world civilization and the position of the Adams family relative to that performance. It was his habit of minute introspection that caused Henry painfully to be aware of his own deficiencies and inconsistencies. And it was John Quincy's failure before the irresistible democratic tide, personified by Andrew Jackson, which first caused both Henry and Brooks to survey the American past with skepticism and to glance at the future with apprehension.

[19] Henry's close association with men of prominence may be examined in H. Adams, *Education.* Brooks' influence on Theodore Roosevelt has been explained by Daniel Aaron, *Men of Good Hope: A Study of American Progressives,* 245–81.

[20] B. Adams, "Introduction," to H. Adams, *Degradation,* 79–86.

The Adams family was historical-minded. It had always been conscious of the past because its members to an amazing degree had helped shape the force and direction of American history. That Henry Adams and Brooks Adams became historians is not a product of coincidence; it was their destiny. In their reaction to history and particularly in their response to the history of their own country, they are at once alike and different. Both perceived disaster as a result of their studies, yet each saw it approaching through different mechanisms. Both were intensely patriotic and interested in the fate of their homeland, yet each adopted an opposite view concerning the necessity of becoming actively involved in public affairs. Both felt like A. E. Housman, "alone and afraid in a world I never made"; yet each reconciled his loneliness in opposite ways. Brooks became the adjusted alien by readopting his native land and attacking viciously those men and forces within it which had made essential the re-adoption. Henry rejected America; he could not become a part of an alien culture, despite the familiarity of nomenclature. He remained aloof from an America whose new *mores* were unacceptable to one whose heart and soul longed for ante bellum days.

In recent years Henry Adams has become the object of much investigation.[21] The fascination which he holds for contemporary society is probably explained by the fact that he has become a symbol of the lost American.[22] He is the *fin-de-siècle* artist who could not find a place for himself amid the great capitalists and materialist thinkers who had come to dominate the American scene. He was not alone with this problem. In fact,

[21] Practically every major work that Henry Adams wrote has been reissued within the past four years. In addition, a multivolume biography by Ernest Samuels promises to be the definitive work. See Samuels, *The Young Henry Adams*, and Samuels, *Henry Adams: The Middle Years*.

[22] H. S. Commager, "Henry Adams," in Hutchinson (ed.), *The Marcus Jernegan Essays in Historiography*. Commager feels that Adams' importance to an understanding of American history lies not so much in what he wrote as what he was.

the most striking characteristic of the literary artist in the United States after the Civil War was his alienation—his sense of rejection by his fellow countrymen.[23] It was perhaps the rejection that prompted the search—a desire for both historical and personal surety. Henry Adams attempted to find an answer for the patchwork puzzle of life which had been created by the gigantic forces that had altered the traditional American façade beyond recognition. His quest convinced him that in the world of the twentieth century certainty was impossible. The universe and the United States along with it were racing ever faster toward their destruction. Only the abysmal ignorance and petty machinations of an impotent mankind lent any comic relief to the tragedy. Whether Henry discovered any formula for his own salvation cannot be discovered; that he felt that the law governing human history insured ultimate degeneration is fact. To the end Henry Adams saw cause only for pessimism.

Like Henry, Brooks Adams also has enjoyed something of a revival.[24] However, the renewal of interest here does not rest on such symbolic foundations. His advice to the modern American is much more concerned with the pressing political and economic realities of the present age. Brooks was passionately concerned with the immediate future of the United States. He too saw peril approaching, but he preached that man was not helpless in the face of such menace. Catastrophe could be averted only if Americans would remove their historical blindfolds and learn the lessons which the past was ready to teach. Naïvely, he was much surer than Henry ever had been that it was possible to reach certitude about history. This trait was uniquely American, and Brooks was brash enough to believe that once he had uncovered the truth for his people there would be unqualified public acceptance. He was willing to fight to

[23] Alfred M. Kazin, *On Native Grounds*, ix.
[24] Brooks has not had his brother's literary revival; however, two recent studies of value are Arthur Beringause, *Brooks Adams*, and Thornton Anderson, *Brooks Adams: Cautious Conservative*.

gain that acceptance. Thus, he never became as pessimistic about the future as Henry. All of his works reflect his dedication to the task of being a modern Paul Revere. It is this seriousness of purpose in addition to the message he conveys which have been the reasons underlying his recent renaissance. Brooks had a solution to the problem of the drift of civilization —an answer based on what he believed was an immutable law of history.

Our concern, then, lies principally with the place that Henry and Brooks Adams occupy in American historiography. We will take as the core of our investigation those writings directly concerned with historical philosophy rather than the factual histories which each man composed. We shall attempt to show that there was more than a fraternal affinity between the two brothers. Their work proceeded along at least one similar vein. Both searched for the law to explain history. Regardless of the validity of the laws they propounded, their trail-blazing has carved for them a special niche among American historians. Henry Adams and Brooks Adams form the necessary bridge between the advocates of purely scientific history and the pragmatic revolutionaries. As is the case with all connecting devices, one can see in their work both the past and the future. They were an integral and essential link in guiding the destiny of American historiography.

3.

Henry *cAdams: The Search*

THE NATURE OF HISTORY

THROUGHOUT THE LONG YEARS that Henry Adams sought the elusive key which would unlock the door of the past, he was forced to come to some conclusions about the nature of history and the historical process. It was most essential that a philosophy of history be founded upon a base that was recognizable and sound. One should not allow the Adams' use of irony and air of detached cynicism to obscure the earnestness with which he attempted to define history. It is difficult to believe that he ever really considered the study of the past to be an occupation suitable only for the mentally indolent.

A fundamental problem was to select a starting point—some place in the course of human development where it might be said that history began. His first inclination was to solve this problem like a philosopher rather than a historian and choose the universe itself as an appropriate beginning. The nature of creation coupled with the nature of reality were problems as much for the historian as the philosophical investigator. However, it was soon apparent that the tools available to the former were far more limited. History had to be content with human evidence, and Adams deferred to the limitation, although noting that he "did not lack the wish to be transcen-

35

dental."[1] Later, when the shadows of the tomb were clearly visible, he would return to his original desire and postulate eternity as the proper point for the inauguration of historical studies. But for the moment he compromised with rationality and decided that history began when man raised himself to the use of an inflected language.[2]

Once this selection had been made it was necessary to determine what were the significant markers which had manifested themselves along the road which stretched from barbarism to the nineteenth century. What was pure history and what was only ephemeral? Certainly, not everything which had occurred at any particular time in the past must be classified as history. If the converse were true, then the historian was overwhelmed before he could begin. Adams was quick to perceive that the problem of selectivity was a crucial one which had been solved in different times in different ways. St. Augustine had seen history as an unfolding of a divine plan leading to the City of God; Hegel viewed the past as a vague foreshadowing of the national spirit; in Adams' own day German historiography had placed great emphasis on the development of institutions, although the latter had been debauched into turning "history into Germany."[3] Thus, since all historians were subject to some kind of determinist influence, the answer could not be discovered in their writings. The novice had to look within himself and then at history. There would be no guarantee that what he discovered would be any more valid than a thousand other discoveries had been, but it would be his own.

Adams, after a lifetime of introspection and investigation, decided that the nature of history was chaos. It was without pattern. He had always felt this intuitively, and fifty years of scholarship only confirmed his initial feeling. His researches

[1] H. Adams, *Education*, 63.
[2] H. Adams "Letter," in *Degradation*, 240.
[3] H. Adams to Frederic B. Luquiens, in Ford, *Letters*, II, 591–92.

into medieval law, while teaching at Harvard, had instructed him in the futility of proving historical sequence, because others looking at a similar set of facts "saw something quite different." His monumental study of the Jefferson and Madison administrations was an experiment at attempting to "fix for a familiar moment a necessary sequence of human movement."[4] It too failed to convince him that a discernible pattern could be objectively ascertained in the multiplicity of events which constituted history. Writing to J. Franklin Jameson, Adams declared that history was a "Chinese play without end and without lesson," and he offered this as his reason for leaving the ranks of the professional historians.[5] Finally, after he had suggested a theory of history in which the central element was chaos and unpredictability, he would remember his earlier wanderings with more bitterness than humor. It had been wasted effort. He recalled the failure of many, himself included, to distinguish between history and the historical method. Learning the Ranke approach to history was no better than intuition in solving the problem of historical reality. History remained a "tangled skein that one may take up at any point, and break when one has unravelled enough; but complexity precedes evolution."[6]

No single method for arriving at historical truth was possible for all situations. Adams, himself, had gained perspective through a variety of mechanisms. The seminar method, which he had introduced so successfully at Harvard, had certainly done much to increase the world's knowledge concerning the origin of Anglo-Saxon legal practices. But a comprehension of the cathedral age in France involved a much less accepted technique. Here the historian seemed to gain more by the ordinary use of his senses than through any dissection of documents

---

[4] H. Adams, *Education*, 382.
[5] November 17, 1896, in Ford, *Letters*, II, 119.
[6] *Ibid.*, 302.

and ancient manuscripts. When his senses had been overcome by the multitude of colors, the enormous pretensions of Gothic architecture, and the interweaving of artistry and religion, then he came to an intellectual understanding of the times. The magnificent cathedral at Chartres was more meaningful to Henry Adams' feeling for the Middle Ages than all of the documents which illustrated the growth of trade or the contents of the Athanasian creed.[7] Whereas a series of incontrovertible statistics might well explain one era, only poetry or illusion could perform the same service for another epoch.

Also the choice of material used to explain any historical period depended largely on the manner in which one intended to write his history. If the narrative approach was to be employed, emphasis would have to be placed on personality or the dramatic event, without too much regard for their relative importance. Conversely, if history was to be written as a scientific treatise, stress was needed on institutional development, social forces, and economic factors. Adams employed both techniques and was never completely satisfied with either. His artistic side constantly urged him to consider history as drama with the world as its stage; at the same time the part of him that was scientist questioned the reliability of the dramatic approach and demanded that history be based on concrete evidence. The past must be constructed so that the present and the future became intelligible. This task required precision and factual data.

Thus there existed within the mind of Henry Adams a fundamental dichotomy concerning the nature of history which is readily observable in everything that he wrote. Indeed, it is part of his charm, an element in the fascination which he continues to exercise on the inquiring reader. But aside from the literary implications of this intellectual dilemma, his failure

[7] H. Adams, *Mont-Saint-Michel and Chartres*, 247. (Hereafter cited as H. Adams, *Mont-Saint-Michel*.)

to arrive at an historical synthesis formulated on an explainable pattern had the profoundest consequences for both his own viewpoint and for the American historical profession. The recognition by Adams that history was paradox, confusion, disorder, and chaos not only saturated his own philosophy with pessimism but also discouraged others from attempting to solve the enigma of Clio with a single scheme. It is more than coincidence that the two most notable efforts in recent years to explain the nature of history have come from Germany and England and not from America.[8]

The true nature of history, then, to Henry Adams was chaos without meaning. In the final analysis it is the rational aspect of his nature that triumphs over the romantic, although the victory was never complete. These two elements, which are perpetually at war in most of humanity, were especially pronounced in him. They are essential tools to understanding both the man and the history that he wrote. He was never really able to divorce himself from noting the tragedy of mankind, ensnared in the spider's web of senseless multiplicity. The chronicler of the human story must, of necessity, "define his profession as the science of human degradation."[9] Within such a framework Adams was willing to make definite observations about both the potentialities and the limitations of the individual historian.

In any determination of what Henry Adams believed to be important rules and guideposts for the historian to follow in practicing his craft, it is important to note immediately that he never laid down an unchanging credo. Rather, as his own work developed and as he gained additional experience, his concept of what constituted the rules of the game often changed. At times the change was radical enough to be in di-

[8] Oswald Spengler, *The Decline of the West;* Arnold J. Toynbee, *A Study of History.*
[9] H. Adams, "Letter," in *Degradation,* 191.

rect contradiction with earlier statements. On other occasions the transformation was more subtle. But always there was adequate motivation for any altering or discarding of previous tenets.

Early in his career, while editor of the *North American Review*, Adams had announced a set of four rules which he felt mandatory for the historian. Originally designed as a gentle reprimand for George Bancroft, they convey what Adams considered the cardinal obligations for the writer of history. They were: the historian should always strive to maintain a judicial mind, the historian should never "hurry" his labors, the historian must acknowledge the limit of his materials, and the historian must always attempt to gauge accurately the impact of the individual personality upon history.[10] However, even the conscientious application of these principles did not assure the historian that his labors would result in any appreciable illumination of the past. As he traveled deeper and deeper into the mystery of previous human experiences, his road became more alien and remote. Yet,

> . . . the historian has no choice but to go on alone. Even in his own profession few companions offer help, and his walk soon becomes solitary, leading further and further into a wilderness where twilight is short and the shadows are dense.[11]

What did Adams mean by asserting that the historian must possess a judicial mind? Is he implying that the student of history must not let himself become inflamed with a spirit of partisanship, or is he inferring that the historian must always remain passively neutral? Can the historian synthesize or generalize? These are processes which most certainly include the use of moral judgment and the assessment of values. Undoubt-

[10] H. Adams, Review of *History of the United States* by George Bancroft, *North American Review*, Vol. CXX (April, 1875), 424–32.
[11] H. Adams, *Education*, 395.

edly Adams meant that the historian must not become an advocate; he would not deny him the right and duty of presenting his history as he saw it. To forbid accurate appraisals of men and events would be unnecessary emasculation. Perhaps he best expressed his feelings on the subject when he noted that "historians and students should have no sympathies or antipathies."[12] Indeed, Adams had almost unqualified praise for the work of Francis Parkman, commenting especially on the completeness and impartiality of the latter's *Montcalm and Wolfe*.[13]

If impartiality was a primary objective, a necessary corollary was that the historian should have enough time for thorough research and unhurried reflection. Historical conclusions were as dependent upon mature thinking as were the meditations of philosophers. Adams' chief criticism of George Bancroft was that his works failed to show any internal evidence of systematized analysis. "The subjects he treats," said Adams, "deserve scientific analysis, and it will be a disgrace to let such a work go out as the measure of our national scholarship."[14] It was not the function of the historian to be either a compiler or a popularizer. Instead, the true student of history must devote his attention to determining the exact nature of the period he is studying. Another generation may build upon this foundation and make popular the results of such research. In his own investigations into American history he never yielded to the temptation to publish more rapidly than prudence counseled. And his great study of the Jefferson and Madison administrations still constitutes as meaningful a contribution to scholarship as has been produced by an American historian. Despite the fact that this twelve-volume study of the United States from 1800 to 1815 was the result of careful research and pains-

[12] *Ibid.*, 438.
[13] H. Adams to Francis Parkman, December 21, 1884, in *Henry Adams and His Friends: A Collection of His Unpublished Letters*, ed. by Harold D. Cater, 133-34. (Hereafter cited as Cater, *Friends*.)
[14] H. Adams to Lewis Henry Morgan, October 3, 1875, in *ibid*, 70.

taking analysis, it has serious limitations, imposed by both the limit of materials and the personality of the writer.

Adams insisted that the historian must admit to himself and to the public the boundaries of his knowledge. The Ranke ideal of a total reconstruction of the past was not capable of actual realization; however, as an ideal toward which the historian must strive, it was useful and instructive. The historian always had to make a distinction between the ideal and what was possible, and it was most essential that he be cognizant of the gap between the two. Moreover, in attempting to understand the past, the writer had to develop a sense of historical-mindedness —a recapturing of the spirit of the times on its own terms. Adams was adamant in his demand that historians fully comprehend the spirit of the age about which they were writing. His own ability to make the mental adjustment of transcending centuries in order that the forgotten years might once again come alive in all their vividness is readily seen in his *Mont-Saint-Michel and Chartres.*

To gain insight into the spirit of the Middle Ages, "one must live deep into the eleventh century."[15] There must be more of a profound comprehension of the great cathedrals than a modern critique of Gothic architecture. Understanding the symbols of an age was an essential preface to understanding the age itself. The symbols and myths which man creates are often the best clues to the temper and reality of any given historical era. Sitting in front of the legendary windows of Chartres, Henry Adams discovered his senses overpowered with all of the vibrancy and delicate nuances of the twelfth century. With an attitude of adoration this pilgrim from the nineteenth century observed:

> Anyone can feel it who will only consent to feel like a child.
> . . . your mind held in the grasp of the strong lines and shadows

15 H. Adams, *Mont-Saint-Michel,* 11.

42

of the architecture; your eyes flooded with the autumn tones of the glass; your ears drowned with the purity of the voices; one sense reacting upon another until sensation reaches the limits of its range.[16]

Unless one approached history in this manner and then coupled his intuitive insight into the spirit of the age with a rigid scientific anaylsis, his history would be no more revealing than the legends and myths he sought to explain. Nor must he forget that history is inextricably interwoven with the human personality—an entity which was the most difficult to ascertain and about which Adams had conflicting ideas.

There is a definite ambivalence in Adams' opinions concerning the importance of the individual in his relationship to the entire historical picture. His advice to Bancroft on the necessity of taking personality into account has already been noted; yet Adams' own *History* was obviously a depicting of a society largely at the mercy of impersonal forces which the leading statesmen of the time were powerless to control. Jefferson, who was strong, and Madison, who was weak, were both impotent in the face of the impending Anglo-American collision. The forces of environment, economics, and the cultural milieu are those presented as leading inevitably to 1812. But an arresting individual like Albert Gallatin or John Randolph never failed to intrigue Adams, and enough doubt remained in his mind about the importance of such men that he wrote biographies of each.

While he remained undecided about personality impact,

---

[16] *Ibid.*, 193–94. Adams never made any claim that historical-mindedness came easily. It was a difficult and laborious procedure. Toward the end of his life he stated that "although my own special branch as a teacher, nearly forty years ago, was the middle-ages, I always despaired of touching the artistic side, in the lecture room, because it is quite impossible for our society, young or old, to get its intellectual processes back to the state of mind in which society naturally expressed itself." H. Adams to Luquiens, July 5, 1910, in *Ford, Letters*, II, 544–45.

Adams was firm in his opinion that heroes were never as significant as many historians considered them to be. He had little patience with the worship of Thomas Carlyle, feeling that throughout history heroes had largely neutralized each other. He excoriated E. A. Freeman for excessive adulation of Alfred the Great and cautioned that such worship could only result in a prostitution of the historian's critical faculty.[17] The notion that any single man had altered significantly the general movement of history was repugnant to a man who was in the process of developing a dynamic theory of history in which human initiative would be considered as only a single manifestation of the dying energy in a dead universe. The individual in history appealed to the artistic or aesthetic side of Adams' nature, but he was too much the student of geology and physics to accept with any credence an axiom of history which posited the importance of heroes. In the conflict of scientist and artist the former usually triumphed, but not without some misgivings.

It would be remiss to omit from any discussion of Adams' concepts about the nature of history a review of what he thought about the general ability of historians and of the profession itself. Generally, he spoke with a good deal of bitterness toward the craft of which he was a leading practitioner. Much of what he said may be discounted and attributed to his well-known habit of exaggerating in order to stimulate thinking and controversy; nevertheless, a certain element of honesty pervades his assertions, and they occur too frequently to be ignored.

Adams was especially hard on the professional historian, who, he felt, had a greater responsibility than did the amateur. Often he despaired of discovering an intelligent historian, "if one should happen to exist."[18] He argued vigorously with Francis

17 H. Adams to William James, July 27, 1882, in Cater, *Friends*, 121; H. Adams, Review of *History of the Norman Conquest* by E. A. Freeman, *North American Review*, Vol. CXVIII (January, 1874), 181.
18 H. Adams, *Mont-Saint-Michel*, 45. See also, H. Adams to Francis Parkman, December 21, 1884, in Cater, *Friends*, 133–34. In this letter Adams makes

Parkman over the seeming inability of the modern historian to make comparisons, to draw analogies, or to broaden his studies to more than one branch of history.[19] He complained of the historiographical poverty of his times. No historian had ever been able to explain the fall of Rome, and this seemed inexcusable. Students were ignorant and helpless before the imponderable contradictions that were Rome; and, when confronted with the problem, they resorted to stereotyped formulas such as time-sequence which to Adams was "the last refuge of helpless historians."[20] Seldom was he visibly impressed with the works of his colleagues, but when he did find merit he was generous in his praise. Sir Henry Maine was one who received an accolade for breaking the tradition of British ignorance and perceiving the continuity of institutions. What Adams appreciated in Maine was his ability to see that England did have a history that antedated the Norman Conquest.[21] George Trevelyan was another of whom he approved, although it might be suspected that Adams had more respect for Trevelyan's pleasing style than for the depth of his research.[22]

He was impatient with those who were willing to accept without reservation or independent investigation questionable historical data which had acquired the aura of truth because of

some interesting and revealing comments on the stature of English historians at the time: "The English are just now poorly off. Except Gardiner and Lecky I know of no considerable English historians besides the old war-horses, Freeman and Froude. My favorite John Green was the flower of my generation; and in losing him, I lost the only English writer of history whom I loved personally and historically." Another stricture on the poverty of English historiography may be found in H. Adams, *Mont-Saint-Michel*, 230–31.

[19] H. Adams to Lewis Henry Morgan, March 29, 1876, in Cater, *Friends*, 78.

[20] H. Adams, *Education*, 91. By "time-sequence" Adams was referring to the common historical practice of arranging events in their proper chronological relationship and then deducing a cause and effect formula from the sequence.

[21] H. Adams, Review of *Village Communities* by Sir Henry Maine, *North American Review*, Vol. CXIV (January, 1872), 196–99.

[22] H. Adams to Charles Milnes Gaskell, March 1, 1899, in Ford, *Letters*, II, 223.

repetition. In fact, the young Henry Adams made his first excursion into scholarship to correct the misconceptions and legends concerning Captain John Smith. He demonstrated equal dissatisfaction with historians who attempted to impose upon history a predetermined arrangement which assumed a silent relation of cause and effect. Sarcastically he suggested that should historians be confronted with their childlike assumptions, they "would probably reply, with one voice, that they had never supposed themselves required to know what they were talking about."[23] Historians were too eager to seize upon some convenient hypothesis which had the sanctity of tradition, and they were often too blind or too inert to struggle with unknown quantities. As examples of problems seldom contemplated, he cited the unexpected revelations of human nature, the influence of women in history, the elements involved in historical proof, and the consequences of timidity in a social or political group.[24] The state of historiography was impoverished, and Adams saw little hope that it would acquire the nourishment which would enable it to live. Just as he ultimately saw only chaos in history, so also he perceived only decay and confusion among her adherents. The profession was saturated with ennui, doubt, and lack of direction. A renaissance was in order.

RELATIVISM AND THE ABSOLUTE

The search which Henry Adams made for a universal law to explain and organize historical data took him into practically every realm of historiography. He was in contact with all of the various explanations and philosophies of history that had been offered, from the cyclical notions of Plato to the scientific speculations of Buckle and Comte. In a mind that was by

[23] H. Adams, *Education*, 382.
[24] H. Adams, *Mont-Saint-Michel*, 55, 279; H. Adams, *Education*, 192, 353.

nature reflective and open, it is not surprising that much of what it encountered was accepted with some alteration or amplification. Thus, it would be an almost insuperable task to delineate each and every idea which contributed to the totality of Adams' historical philosophy and to his eventual conclusion that a law for history was, indeed, possible. Instead, we shall attempt to isolate those forces which play the dominant roles.

There were three fundamental elements which, both by negative and positive means, influenced and directed the historical thinking of Henry Adams. These three elements, generalized for purposes of simplification, were relativism, Darwinism, and religion. Their importance, relative to each other, in producing the completed philosophy was probably in ascending order, with religion being more significant than either Darwinism or relativism. It was characteristic of Adams that, in essence, he rejected the ultimate implications of all three. His was not a historical concept which was based solely on any single idea; nor was it indebted to any single individual. Rather it was a composite, taking and rejecting of what it pleased until a unique and extremely individualistic structure had been erected. Within this structure the use of irony and either assumed or actual skepticism were constantly visible, often obscuring the exact nature of the structure itself. Consequently, he who would analyze and examine the interweaving of Adams' ideas must be alert to the danger of confusing the essential with the ephemeral. Another facet to be remembered is the recurrence of ambivalence; Adams always seemed to reach a fixed point by a circuitous route—one which was encumbered by many contradictions. This deviousness, although not artificial, was an integral part of his mind. In fact it became a basic part of his historical scheme. He was never able to reconcile the two sides of his nature; they were both manifest in his personality and in his writings, and they were sharply etched in his opinions concerning the relativity of human experience.

At first glance it might seem futile to suggest that any theory of history which had as its core the formulation of a scientific law could contain a suggestion of relativism. Was not the primary objective of the relativists to discredit any absolute approach to history? How then could Henry Adams be described as being influenced by relativistic doctrines? Not only was Adams addicted to many such nuances, but in certain areas he foreshadowed the work of men like Beard and Becker. Moreover, Adams was often a relativist on the doctrine's own terms, if the conclusions of Chester Destler about the nature of the relativistic creed are taken as accurate. In this creed Destler detected eight fundamental principles: scientific objectivity is unobtainable, truth is always relative to the historian's known biases, the past can never be re-created in its entirety, the finished historical product must be regarded as symbolic rather than factual, history can never be definitive, history must be constantly rewritten, it is the present which dictates the relevance of history, and causality should disappear as a tool of interpretation.[25] Adams was close in principle to many of them, but he was especially convinced that a total re-creation of the past was impossible.

More than once Adams commented on the difficulties in exposing the historical past as it really existed. The crux of the problem lay in the historian's utter dependence upon facts. To the average historian conclusions based on facts were as scientific as the results of a chemical analysis; yet Adams insisted that neither could ever really be sure that their facts were absolute verities. Historical facts lacked surety because of their incompleteness. The result was that "all opinion founded on fact must be error . . . and their relations must be always infinite."[26] This conclusion did not absolve the historian from

[25] Chester M. Destler, "Some Observations on Contemporary Historical Theory," *American Historical Review*, Vol. CV (April, 1950), 503–29.
[26] H. Adams, *Education*, 410.

the responsibility of seeking the truth; however, Adams maintained that he would arrive at truth only at the expense of falsifying his facts. Despite his hatred of complete dependence on so-called factual data, he did believe that an accurate, as opposed to entire, reconstruction was possible. What mattered was not whether details were exact, but whether the whole plan was in scale. The historian's perception and grasp of any period need not be limited by either the scarcity or ambiguity of facts; he does not need all of the data to present a meaningful picture. It is at this juncture that Adams differs radically from the modern relativist who equates truth with entirety.[27] Yet within such a boundary the separate items making up the whole are bound to be incomplete and, hence, relative.

Henry Adams would also assuredly agree with the idea that it is the present which dictates the relevancy of the past. Indeed, it was his preoccupation with the needs of the twentieth century and its potential for catastrophe that impelled the search for a law which might illumine and perhaps eliminate some of the pitfalls awaiting modern society. Writing to an unidentified correspondent, Adams put it this way:

> I need not add that, in all probability, my work as well as all the other historical work of our generation, will probably fail to suit the needs of the twentieth century. We cannot now fully see these needs, but we begin to feel them.[28]

This fact, however, did not necessarily proscribe the validity of the information which was gathered concerning the past,

[27] In the early stage of his development Adams had held out as an ideal the notion of writing an entire history. He had written concerning his researches into United States history of the Jefferson and Madison periods that "I want to tell the whole truth." H. Adams in James Russell Lowell, September 24, 1879, in Cater, *Friends*, 92.

[28] October 6, 1899, in Cater, *Friends*, 480. For expert information about the identity of the recipient of Adams' letter, see the footnote at bottom of the page in Cater, *Friends*, 479.

albeit he did admit the tendency for the present to see the past as a mirror of its own problems and to look into that mirror for possible solutions.

That the past could aid the present and that it was the present which predetermined the significance of special areas in history were ideas to which Adams gave a good amount of credence. There were several illustrations which demonstrated the basic truth of this assertion. Gibbon's treatment of the decline and fall of Rome was notable. In 1789, Adams wrote, "Gibbon ignored the Virgin because . . . religious monuments were out of fashion."[29] The great English historian saw in the past what his own age dictated for him to see. Consequently, he perceived the twin destructive forces of barbarism and Christianity as producing the decline of a civilization which was to Gibbon the equivalent of Rome. Later generations of historians would not be as harsh with the religion of Christ; but Gibbon, writing in a time when all orthodox religion was being attacked by the rationalism of the Enlightenment, reflected the temper of his own times.

Another example was the modern treatment of the Middle Ages in general and the view of medieval poetry in particular. To the medieval mind, the immortal Frankish poem *Roman de la Rose* was the apex of a beautiful and delicate literary tradition. For three hundred years much of medieval verse had been either graceful imitation or variation of the same themes. Nevertheless, "our age calls it false taste, and no doubt our age is right; every age is right by its own standards as long as its own standards amuse it."[30] The problem of evaluation was not in the poetry; it remains constant. Rather, the universe presented itself in different aspects to mankind as it moved. Man is prone to view objects and events from a previously accepted foundation. The differences between 1100 and 1900 lie not in

[29] *Education*, 387.
[30] H. Adams, *Mont-Saint-Michel*, 272.

human nature nor in the appearance of the universe but in what society accepts as its own base. In 1100 that base was provided by the Church and Aristotle; in 1900 the substructure was the laws of legislatures and energy.

It can be easily seen that Henry Adams accepted many, if not all, of the relativistic tenets. Certainly, near the end of his career he had abandoned a strictly Ranke view concerning the possibility of complete historical objectivity. In this development he was paralleled by the Frenchman Renan. Both eventually yielded to the concept that each age re-creates the past in its own image. It does not follow, however, that either accepted the ultimate implication—namely, that the past is totally unknowable. Adams never went as far as Carl Becker, even though he appreciated the depth and profundity of the latter's work. The relativity of history did not alter its meaningfulness. "History could be written in one sense just as easily as in another."[31] He conceded that "past history is only a value of relation to the future"[32] but that its validity could be tested by experiment. If the future conformed to a plan which had predicated the past as its base, then history was useful and, in the best sense, knowable.

The relativistic aspect of Adams' thought was of decisive importance in producing his historical law. It broadened his perspective, made him aware of his own limitations, and provided him a useful tool with which to compare divergent societies. It tempered his earlier didacticism with a subtler appreciation of humanity and humanity's development. Finally, it affected the very nature of the law he developed; for far from being an absolute dictum concerning the movement of human history, the law of Henry Adams acknowledged the relativity of strictly human experience and selected as its starting point not man but the universe which imprisoned him. It is ironic that Henry

[31] H. Adams, "Letter," in *Degradation*, 239.
[32] H. Adams, *Education*, 488.

Adams was unaware of two short scientific treatises, published in 1905 by a young German, Albert Einstein, in which a theory of relativity was applied to that universe Henry had hoped to be absolute.

DARWINISM AND DEGENERATION

Henry Adams had always been captivated by science and scientists. As a young man he had seen the upheavals generated by the revolutions in biology, geology, and physics. As one who remembered the relative agrarian peacefulness of pre-1860 America, he was more than casually aware of the transformation science had wrought in his native land after the Civil War. In a sense *The Education of Henry Adams* was the account of an attempt to comprehend the nature and extent of the changes. When editing the *North American Review*, he had come into personal contact with Sir Charles Lyell and his writings. It was not mere chance that one of the most favorable book reviews Adams ever wrote concerned Lyell's *Principles of Geology*. And the review is notable not only for its favorable treatment of the new geology but also for its revelation that the author was no initiate into geologic mysteries. There was excitement in the strides which science seemed to be making, excitement in the challenges which it offered the traditions of all institutions, and excitement in being part of an age that threatened to outstrip all previous epochs in broadening the intellectual vistas of mankind.

The theory which stimulated the greatest controversy and which fired the imaginations of men in every field was Charles Darwin's hypothesis of biological evolution. Perhaps no other book in history has had such an enormous impact as *The Origin of Species* exercised on the nineteenth-century mind. The notion of evolution, itself, was not especially new; indeed, most biologists had long discarded the concept of spontaneous gen-

HENRY ADAMS, about 1870, when he was an assistant professor in Harvard University.

Courtesy of the Harvard University Archives

eration. The reason for the almost immediate popularity of Darwin was the favorable climate of opinion extant in 1859. In an atmosphere in which public confidence in the literal validity of the Scriptures had been shaken by the higher criticism, in which liberal philosophies unchained by the French Revolution were transforming political and social concepts, and in which science was becoming a respectable member of the arts, there was a willingness to accept what a previous generation would have dismissed without serious examination. Speculative philosophy also seized upon Darwin's evolutionary ideas as possibly possessing the potential not only of explaining the world's biological development but also of providing a rational and workable scheme for determining man's role and significance in the cosmos. The implications of Darwinism were immense for the historian, and Henry Adams was one of the first to probe the new avenues of approach.

Darwinism was a second important force in Adams' search for a law of history, and it influenced the direction of his thought in two significant ways. First, it confirmed his feeling that the historian must look to the sciences for solutions; and, second, his intense disillusionment with progressive evolution led him to assert the idea of degeneration (negative evolution) which became the key to his dynamic theory of history. Again, one must be careful in analyzing the exact posture which Adams maintained, for his own thinking on the subject is replete with innuendo and ambiguity. It is true that Henry Adams rejected evolutionary schemes as applicable to history; it is equally certain that Darwinism left an indelible imprint upon his beliefs and art.

Adams reached Darwin through the door of paleontology instead of biology, through Lyell instead of Herbert Spencer. Consequently, his orientation was never truly Darwinian, and his later objections to evolution as a tool for the historian were objections to the implications made by men like John Fiske.

Both Fiske and Spencer became crusaders in a most enthusiastic manner; Adams was anything but a champion of causes. He had an almost neoclassical distaste for enthusiasm, and the ardor displayed by stout Darwinian advocates repelled his cooler nature. Moreover, Darwinism to the geologist carried connotations unknown to the biological scientist—connotations which were much more mysterious and more difficult to accept. Nevertheless, when evolution first began to attract the attention of American intellectuals, Henry Adams was one of those fascinated by the new theory; and for a while he could be counted among its adherents.

Looking back on what he considered a youthful folly, Adams attributed his original fascination to the fact that so many shocking new theories were being offered for consumption that one took them up simply to be disturbing to the older generation. In addition to natural selection, the atomic theory, the correlation and conservation of energy, the mechanical theory of the universe, and the kinetic theory of gases were absorbed. Furthermore, such ideas were "new and seemed to lead somewhere—to some great generalization which would finish one's clamor to be educated."[33] Here was the real motive: Darwinism might be the key for which Adams was seeking.

Still, the evolutionary key did not seem to open all the doors. Adams could never reconcile Darwinism to all of the objections which seemed immediately to leap to mind. He could see no concrete proof in history of the survival of the fittest nor of natural selection. But by far the greatest obstacle he encountered was the notion that evolution and progress were synonymous.

The notion of progress in history had been a part of historical philosophy since Descartes had constructed a mechanical view of the universe in the seventeenth century. It had received its first concrete statement by Condorcet at the time of the French Revolution, and the nineteenth century had oc-

[33] *Ibid.*, 224.

cupied itself with the attempt to give the doctrine a scientific base. In a sense the factor which made the doctrine so appealing was that it could prove to be a most acceptable substitute for religious faith. To the humanity who rejected the solaces of orthodox Christianity the idea of progress promised a perfectibility which did not rely on divine intervention for its fulfillment. The Darwinian theorem with its emphasis upon the survival of the fittest appeared to substantiate the progressive idea. If Darwin could observe plant and animal life discarding the unfit and developing increasingly hardy and complex forms, should not the historian be able to witness a similar process in mechanics of human development? Man was as much a part of nature as the algae and was subject to the same deterministic natural influences. After a thorough study of history Adams concluded that this theory would not meet the critical challenge; it was obvious, he felt, that mankind had not progressed.

He ascribed the willingness of historians to preach perfectibility to the innate optimism of human nature. Both the individual and society desire to see "its indefinite progress towards perfection." The human ego will not permit it to conceive that man and his works may not be the ultimate in creation. In reality, Adams asserts, the honest historian must perceive degradation rather than progression. The stark reality of history must concern itself with the probable extinction of the species, not with recriminatory debates over origins. This truism was confirmed, he thought, by mundane history and by the laws of thermodynamics. The only true measure of progress was the activity of human thought, and, if one took Plato as a starting point, it was indeed difficult to trace any significant progress to the twentieth century. Moreover, Adams' complete acceptance of Lord Kelvin's theorem, the degradation of energy within the universe, led him to denounce progress on scientific grounds. Thus:

If Thought were actually a result of transforming other energies into one of a higher potential, it must still be equally subject to the laws which governed those energies, and could not be an independent or super-natural force.[34]

Another objection which Adams raised to Darwinism was its dependence on an a priori assumption. Evolution contained a presupposition as imponderable as Paley's inference that "if one found a watch, one inferred a maker."[35] Looking at both biology and history, Adams detected only change; he did not see progress. He granted that a theory of natural selection could account for change, but he denied that it ever dictated the direction of the change. For that accomplishment a shaping influence from the outside was imperative. Inevitably, the historian who attempted to construct a scheme of history which had purpose and direction was forced to adopt an eschatological view and to fit his epistemology into a preconceived framework. The Darwinist differed from St. Augustine only in that he had substituted evolution for God.

Furthermore, to one as complex as Henry Adams the evolutionary hypothesis appeared too simple a formula. It was too all-embracing to account for the infinitely varied phenomena of history. The historian, thought Adams, must not be content with simple explanations; however, the doctrine of evolution had become so pervasive that neither the writer nor the teacher could escape it. It made little difference what alternatives were suggested. History could be treated as a catalogue, a romance, or an evolution; whether the historian either affirmed or denied the doctrine, he would still fall "into all the burning faggots of

[34] H. Adams, "Tendency," in *Degradation*, 128; H. Adams, "Letter," in *Degradation*, 165–66, 182, 216–17. Adams' personal conception of Kelvin's meaning was nonscientific though accurate. In a letter to Gaskell he described his interpretation as a "universe, including our corner of it, flattening steadily, and would in the end flatten out to a dead level where nothing could live." June 6, 1909, in Ford, *Letters*, II, 519.
[35] H. Adams, *Education*, 230.

the pit."[36] Therein lay the real danger to the objective historian. No matter which way he turned he was certain to be infected with this pernicious disease. This intuitive criticism which Adams intended as a warning for others might well have been applied to himself. For despite his conscious rejection of evolution, his own historical work and philosophy often betray the influence of Charles Darwin.

The observations which Henry Adams made on American society after the Civil War depend in a large measure on Darwinist ideas. The spectacular growth of the large corporation, the rise of the "robber baron," and the growing tendency for politicians to be the organs of the business community were cited as examples of the strong prevailing over the weak. The men who organized and controlled the new power elite were products of the forces of nature. They were prime examples of the doctrine that only the fittest survived. Presidential nominations of such men as Grant, Garfield, and Blaine were additional proof that society was "pitilessly sacrificing the weak and deferentially following the strong."[37]

Adams' use of evolution may also be noted in other ways. The methods he used in instructing the course in medieval history at Harvard was basically evolutionary—tracing the growth of institutions as developmental from early primitivism.[38] His belief that throughout history the most appalling waste had been that of the human mind led him to a Darwinian conclusion. "Only the most energetic, the most highly fitted, and the most favored have overcome the friction . . . of inertia."[39] This is pure natural selection. Even in his final rejection of Darwinism a remnant of evolutionary thought remains. What attracted both Darwin and Adams about life was the problem of change. But whereas the Darwinists saw progress in a series of infinite

[36] *Ibid.*, 300.
[37] *Ibid.*, 280.
[38] Merle E. Curti, *The Growth of American Thought*, 568–69.
[39] H. Adams, *Education*, 314.

changes, Adams saw retrogression. In a sense it was the evolutionary postulate of change that caused Henry Adams to renounce the idea of progress in favor of degradation.

Thus, the doctrine of evolution was exceedingly important in the search Henry Adams made for a universal law. That he rejected Darwin does not lessen the importance; rather, it increases it. For had he not so carefully scrutinized the doctrine of evolution, he would never have arrived at an opposing theory. He admitted the debt which he and all historians owed Darwinism when writing to American teachers of history:

> This popular understanding of Darwinism had little to do with Darwin, whose great service,—in the field of history,—consisted by no means in his personal theories either of natural selection, or of adaptation, or of uniform evolution; which might be all abandoned without affecting his credit for bringing all vital processes under the law of development or evolution,— whether upward or downward being immaterial to the principle that all history must be studied as a science.[40]

RELIGION AND SKEPTICISM

The desire to believe was strong in Henry Adams, as it must be in all who undertake to chronicle the record of humanity. It was the very acuteness of his desire which made his inability to achieve a satisfactory religious synthesis all the more poignant. His entire intellectual life was plagued by the conflicting demands of faith and reason, and the same motive which impelled him to scan history for a recognizable law also urged him to seek an active faith in a benevolent God. In fact, it was his search for religious truth that played the dominant role in eventually determining his final verdict on the significance of history.

Adams could never escape from the tyrannies of his Puritan

[40] H. Adams, "Letter," in *Degradation*, 149.

heritage. Struggle as he might, the compulsion to make moral judgments and the desire to fix an absolute standard for all things was strong within him. Rationally, he rejected the inheritance of Calvinism; but emotionally, he made periodic efforts to reclaim a lost religiosity. The intense feeling which permeates *Mont-Saint-Michel and Chartres* is demonstrable evidence of his feeling for the spiritual, although he recognized that the religion of the Middle Ages was dead—a fact which constantly amazed him. "That the most powerful emotion of man, next to the sexual, should disappear" was unbelievable.[41] Yet, Henry Adams, himself, was an example of the thinness of religious feeling in modern times. His break with orthodoxy did not come after long and tedious philosophical meditation; it occurred after the most common and most personal of experiences, the death of a loved one. After the demise of his sister, Adams concluded that "God might be, as the Church said, a Substance, but He could not be a Person."[42] Despite the familiarity of the experience, this was the point from which Adams began his quest for an explanation of human history— a search which began as an attempt to find a replacement for the traditional God and which terminated when the seeker thought he had discovered the substitute, the science of physics. However, along the tortuous road the pilgrim made many detours, one of which nearly returned him to the original position. And it is both ironic and characteristic that once the answer had been found, Henry Adams remained dissatisfied.

Adams defined religion as the "recognition of unseen power which has control of man's destiny." Every man recognized the incomprehensibility of his presence in the universe and felt a need to justify his existence. This was the price which man had to pay for the gift of self-consciousness. But what man had identified as the unseen power had been illusion, a combination

[41] H. Adams, *Education*, 34.
[42] *Ibid.*, 288–89.

of superstition and fetish which, in reality, was but a reflection of the mind's own images. The transition from polytheism to monotheism was not a great revolution; it was only an acceleration in the same direction. "From first to last the fetish idea inhered in the thought; the idea of an occult power to which obedience was due."[43] Such fetishes were satisfactory only for as long as man remained unscientific. Once mankind began to unwind some of the riddles of nature, there had to be a re-evaluation of the function of religion; its teleology had to be reinterpreted.

The great object of the Church and religion had been to offer a pattern of unity in a universe which was a maze of complexity.[44] Indeed, the Church had been the only institution that had affirmed unity with any conviction. In the Western world the organism which had proclaimed a doctrine of unity had been the Christian Church. It had denounced the fetishes of paganism as heathen; yet when Adams viewed the panorama of Christianity he saw only that it had simply coalesced all the symbols of paganism into an even more occult image, the cross. It could be used as potently as any golden calf:

> The symbol represented the sum of nature—the Energy of modern science—and society believed it to be as real as x-rays; perhaps it was! The emperors used it like gunpowder in politics; the physicians used it like rays in medicine; the dying clung to it as the quintessence of force, to protect them from the forces of evil on their road to the next life.[45]

Thus Christianity had been an enormous failure. It had

[43] H. Adams, "The Rule of Phase Applied to History," in *Degradation*, 288–89.

[44] Adams uses the terms "unity" and "complexity" throughout his works to indicate an attitude of polarity. In most instances unity is equivalent to meaningfulness and complexity to incomprehensibility. The terms, when used here, carry those connotations.

[45] H. Adams, *Education*, 479.

posited unity on outworn premises and at the sacrifice of reason. And it had annihilated reason when it had embraced intellectualism. True religion was love; never was it logic. After almost two thousand years the world was as vicious and bloodthirsty as ever. Christianity lost its essence when it chose Aquinas over St. Francis. There was some justification for attempting to reach God by spiritual methods alone, but to reach God by the syllogisms of Aristotelian deduction was unthinkable. The Church had been too much concerned with the knowledge that latent skepticism lurks behind all faith, and to overcome skeptical objections she had stooped to employ reason, the weapon of the enemy. That the instrument would eventually be turned on the Church was inevitable. The modern age's lack of faith was something it had inherited from religion. In attempting to prove unity the Church had only confirmed complexity.

Since the Church had labored so tenaciously to establish a system of unity, Adams believed that a close inspection of that period in history when Christianity had dominated the whole of society was a necessary starting place for the historian who was seeking his way out of the morass of the modern world. It was not difficult to make a choice; the thirteenth century stood like a beacon. It was a century in which the cross was supreme as the symbol of man's relationship to God; it was the era of the great cathedrals; it was the age of Thomas Aquinas, of Abélard, of Eleanor of Aquitane, of Blanche of Castile. It was the golden time to Catholic historians, who often termed it the "greatest of centuries." In short, if there had ever been a time when man felt safe and secure in a universe run for his benefit by the loving Creator, it was at this time—the fruition of the Middle Ages.

The keys to understanding this superlative century were to be found in its religious art and in its devotion to the Virgin. Henry Adams claimed that religious art was the hallmark of any society; it was the true measure of human sincerity. Certainly the century of the great cathedrals was a luxurious example of a high expression of religious feeling. The century's adoration of Mary also permeated its art and literature. There could be no real comprehension of the spirit of the age unless there was a realization of the place that Mary had occupied. To Adams, who asserted convincingly that the Church had always been a feminine institution,[46] the Virgin's enthronement was not surprising. Yet the skeptical Adams, who thought that his investigation of medieval unity had been undertaken in a spirit of purely scientific inquiry, who had come to the shrines of the Mother of Christ in order to determine the source of her attraction, was caught by the charm of a past that was forever lost, and himself became a worshipper at the feet of Mary. Although he was finally able to wrench himself away from the spell of Chartres, he never forgot its magic. Intellectually, he returned to the twentieth century; but a part of his soul remained, like a lone vigil candle, to honor the woman in the vastness and beauty of the cathedral which had been built in her honor.

The unit constructed by the medieval world, according to Adams, was best typified in the cathedral and in the *Summa Theologica* of Thomas Aquinas. Both seemed to be the highest expressions of energy and will. Undoubtedly, it was the promise of eternity which provided the stimulant necessary to the construction of both. The cathedral was a physical attempt of small man to grasp the infinite; all of the Gothic elaborations were directed toward this end:

> You may, if you like, figure in it a mathematic formula of infinity—the broken arch, our finite idea of space; the spire, pointing, with its converging lines, to unity beyond space; the sleepless, restless thrusts of the vaults, telling the unsatisfied,

[46] H. Adams, *Mont-Saint-Michel*, 306; H. Adams, *Education*, 446.

incomplete, overstrained effort of man to rival the energy, intelligence, and purpose of God.[47]

The great work of Aquinas was the intellectual counterpart of the cathedral. It too was the product of great energy, and it also attempted to construct an edifice which would lead man to God. Its relentless logic placed the Creator within a rational framework and made Him conform to human standards.

Whereas thirteenth-century man saw the unity of the Divine in such a society, Adams was more impressed with the energy which that society had expended. Energy was the great force the historian had to understand if he were to understand history. Already he had concluded that the most prominent symbol of an age was one which expressed the era's energy concept. For the twentieth century that symbol was the dynamo; in the thirteenth it was the Virgin. When one compared the power which each had exercised over human thought and development, the conclusion was inevitably reached that the Virgin had exuded more of an "attraction over the human mind than all the steam-engines and dynamos ever dreamed of."[48] Adams was intrigued with the symbol of Mary. He reasoned that she had outstripped the Trinity in winning worship because she embodied the sex symbols of paganism with the love tokens of Christianity. Mary thus became to Henry Adams the supreme example of unity. From her domination to that of the modern dynamo had been a descent from the security of unity to the chaos of multiplicity.

To accept Adams' final explanation of Mary on his own terms of pure physics would be to miss part of the real significance that the Virgin held for him and his search for an acceptable law of history. It may be that the emotionalism with which he embraced the study of the Virgin was an escape from the scientific determinism which had replaced in the modern era the faith

[47] *Ibid.,* 115.
[48] H. Adams, *Education,* 384–85.

of his Puritan ancestors. The Mother of Jesus may have been the compensation for a lost religion. Undoubtedly, he did somewhat misunderstand the role of Mary as the intercessor in medieval society, but there is little truth to the charge that he did not understand either Mary or medievalism and that *Mont-Saint-Michel and Chartres* is sheer blasphemy. Adams understood the Middle Ages far better than most of his critics, and it is certain that Mary came to represent something more than a substitution for science. Yet, there was a parallel between the Virgin and the dynamo, between religion and science. It was the exploitation of this relationship which represented the chief influence that religious study exercised on Adams' development of a scientific law for historical study.

Science and religion resembled each other in a variety of ways. Both attempted to explain the universe and the energies within it. Both attempted to isolate the universal substance which was the prime motor of life. The scientist studied it in the laboratory; the devout worshipped it in church. Each was alike in its dogmatisms, and in its devotion to a set of shibboleths. If it were true that the Church had "raised ignorance to a faith and degraded dogma to heresy," it was equally true that the doctrine of evolution had survived without evolving.[49] The terminology of science was as mystical and as unintelligible to the layman as the language of theology. Finally, both had as an ultimate goal the creation of order out of disorder, of unity out of complexity, of law out of incoherence. And both had failed. Darwin knew no more than Aquinas. When Lord Kelvin announced the second law of thermodynamics, he was saying to his fellow scientists much the same thing that the Church had said to Abélard: "Where we know so little, we had better hold our tongue."[50]

Henry Adams followed three important paths in reaching

49 *Ibid.*, 401.
50 H. Adams, *Mont-Saint-Michel*, 325–26.

the law of degeneration. He rejected relativism, Darwinism, and religion as sole guardians of truth, but each had an incalculable influence on the shaping of his thought. In his own way he had arrived at an answer which was as devoid of hope for man as it was for a universe doomed to eternal sterility. The world remained a riddle, and as he grew softly into old age, Adams understood even himself only in form of fable. As life drained from him, he must have recalled with pain the feeling that had swept over him when he left the cathedral at Chartres. The image remained intact: the majestic queen, surrounded by her devoted and mute entourage, "looking down from a deserted heaven, into an empty church, on a dead faith."[51]

[51] Richard P. Blackmur, "Henry Adams: Three Late Moments," *Kenyon Review*, Vol. II (Winter, 1940), 29; H. Adams, *Mont-Saint-Michel*, 213.

4.

Brooks Adams: The Search

Brooks adams had the happy faculty of being able to convince himself of the complete truth of his opinions, once those opinions had been formed. He was not plagued with self-doubt, as was his brother Henry, nor was he given to critical re-evaluation or reinterpretation of his theories. Once he had decided that a certain set of facts established a pattern, he only discovered supporting data in subsequent investigations. He established archetypes and thereafter never questioned their validity. Consequently, his presentation is always straightforward. There is no deviousness, no linguistic trickery, no concession to literary protocol. Brooks Adams believed fervently that he had uncovered the truth that had been hidden in history. His own work, he conceived, was to awaken his countrymen to this truth so that they might be forewarned concerning their individual and collective fates. He was a man with a mission; he was a modern Paul Revere, rushing to inform America that it was not the British who were coming but rather the steady march of inevitable decay. It was a prophecy deeply imbedded in the nature of the historical process.

For Brooks Adams there was only one reason for studying history, and that was the possibility of discovering a law which by explaining the past might also serve as a guide for the future. An accumulation of facts for the sake of facts was abhorrent. Antiquarianism was a pursuit without meaning, suitable only for the mentally indigent. The facts of history only acquired value when enough had been collected to suggest a cause and effect sequence. Then a generalization or a law could be deduced, and by his own definition, a law occurred when "certain phenomena have been found to succeed each other with sufficient regularity to enable us to count with reasonable certainty on their recurrence in a determined order."[1]

Adams did admit that the historian whose livelihood was dependent upon the sale of his works had to take into consideration commercial and literary aspects as well as educational and scientific factors. In fact, most of the great work in history had been done because of commercial necessity; however, if the historian was an honest craftsman the results would be the same. History, whether written from educational or financial motives, could be instructive and rewarding. The reward should always be additional insight into the multiplicity of events which would allow a meaningful pattern or law to emerge.

Certainly, the desire to discern the meaning of history was the principal object of Adams' own investigations. He was not concerned with presenting all of the facts or with attempting a total reconstruction of the past on its own terms. What he did was to present a working hypothesis or theory and then illustrate it with a sampling of historical facts. His motive was always to warn, to instruct, to make the public aware of what fate had already decided. "I use history as little as possible and only as illustration."[2] In essence Brooks Adams was more the

[1] Brooks Adams, *The New Empire*, xviii. Adams was most insistent on this point. "Save as an amusement for the antiquary, history and economics which deal with the past without reference to the present have no significance. Research for its own sake is futile. The only practical value which these studies have is the light they throw upon the present and the future." *Ibid.*, xvii.

[2] Quoted in Daniel Aaron, "Brooks Adams: The Unusable Man," *New England Quarterly*, Vol. XXI (March, 1948), 31–32.

polemicist than the historian. History was only a tool (the most basic one to be sure) by which man could achieve an understanding of the meaning of his own experience.

It was quite logical to Adams that history would be able to give answers, for he viewed history as but one of an infinite variety of forces making up the universe. Society was but another organism, which operated like other organisms on various mechanical principles. Viewed so mechanistically, historians by their studies should be able to "learn enough of those principles to enable us to view, more intelligently than we otherwise should, the social phenomena about us."[3] Nor were these principles obscure. Just as Newton and Galileo had come to conclusions based on the most obvious of evidence, so the historian could accomplish the same thing. Brooks Adams was never reluctant to draw what he inferred to be a self-evident conclusion. What to others might appear unintelligible seemed perfectly clear to him. When he compared the political philosophies of Edmund Burke and Charles Fox, he came quickly to the point. Burke was the slave of prejudices and affectations, while Fox was "broad and vigorous enough to comprehend that there are movements among men which may be guided, but which cannot be subdued by force."[4] There was no hesitation here, no thorough appraisal of the many social and cultural forces at work. Similarly, in noting the disappearance of the Roman husbandman and soldier from the stage of history, Adams commented that the reason was obvious. "Nature had turned against him; the task of history is but to ascertain his fate."[5]

The nature of history, then, could be as accurately determined as the nature of any physical-chemical process. All life, whether it be the life of an individual organism or the life of

[3] B. Adams, *The Theory of Social Revolutions*, 203.
[4] B. Adams, "The Last State of English Whiggery," *Atlantic Monthly*, Vol. XLVII (April, 1881), 571–72.
[5] B. Adams, *The Law of Civilization and Decay*, 25.

Brooks Adams had his picture made, along with the rest of his class at Harvard, in 1870.

Courtesy of the Harvard University Archives

a social organism, was related to a basic philosophical problem. The problem to which Adams referred was "man's eternal struggle with a restless nature to maintain order and some approximation to social unity amidst universal and endless change."[6] When one accepted that all historical movement was society's attempt to solve this problem, one had taken the first step toward perceiving the meaning inherent in historical experience. The next step was to conclude that man, himself, was an integral part of the processes of nature. He was not above nature; rather, he reflected it in all of its contradictions and diversities. The more freedom the individual was allowed, the more would he be an accurate reflection of the complexity of the universe.[7] Thus, the starting points of Adams' concepts concerning the nature of history were the universe and man. But they were not separate elements; they were contained within each other, and neither was sensible if studied in isolation. Man was only a manifestation of an energy, and man's history was likewise the record of how that energy operated. What the historian had to do was study the energy and discover what law it followed in its dispersal.

At first glance the expenditure of social energy seemed to follow no particular pattern. Civilizations rose abruptly and even more suddenly began to decline. The destinies of nations often seemed as if they were decided by the whims of fate or the chances of war. Humanity's progress in both morals and technology continued at an uneven pace. Men lived and died without any readily apparent reason. There seemed to be nothing but the sheerest nonsense in history. Yet, on closer scrutiny Adams detected that nothing in history was accidental.

[6] B. Adams, "Can War Be Done Away With?" *Papers and Proceedings, American Sociological Society*, Vol. X (1916), 103.

[7] B. Adams, "Introduction," to H. Adams, *Degradation*, 109. This was why Brooks believed that of all forms of government democracy was least likely to provide order and security. Democracy reflected in the political life the tremendous variety of forces which made the physical universe seem chaotic.

Men and society moved in "obedience to an impulsion as automatic as the impulsion of gravitation."[8] They were mere automatons moved by forces over which they had no control. They were a part of the processes of nature and nothing more, and since the evident and unique characteristic of nature was movement, it logically followed that the perpetual motion of history was a part of the universal law.

The very nature of history, therefore, was law—a law which had its foundations in nature. It was a fixed law which moved along predictable lines. Individuals, nations, and civilizations obeyed the same set of regulations. History may be studied scientifically "until the origin of the phenomena of the twentieth century may be traced back to the murky past which preceded the pyramid of Cheops, and human development may be presented as a mechanical whole."[9] The same law, when discovered, would explain such diverse events as Colbert's adoption of mercantilism for France in the seventeenth century or the rise of modern Russia and Germany to the status of world powers. Everything was obedient to law, even the action of mind. The cause was followed by the consequence "with the precision that the earth moves around the sun."[10]

Although Brooks Adams had approached the study of history from the viewpoint that everything was a part of nature, he held that the idea that history was mechanistic would be inevitably reached regardless of the method. For the historian who believed in a beneficent Creator, Adams saw as inescapable the deduction that such a Being thinks according to scientific laws. One could not deny, he contended, the validity of the law of gravitation. If God was responsible for the universe, then He was also responsible for the immutability of its laws. There was demonstrable proof that nature conformed to scien-

8 B. Adams, *The Theory of Social Revolutions*, 3.

9 B. Adams, *The New Empire*, 4.

10 B. Adams, *The Emancipation of Massachusetts: The Dream and the Reality*, 211. (Hereafter cited as B. Adams, *The Emancipation*.)

tific determinants. Therefore, a benevolent God was also a scientific one, and there was no reason to believe that the laws for history were any less fixed than the laws for falling bodies. Nor could there be a rational division for the behavioral characteristics of physical and mental phenomena. Moreover, it was thought, either conscious or unconscious, which constituted history. "If intellectual phenomena are involved in a regular sequence, history, like matter, must be governed by law."[11]

Thus, for Brooks Adams there was absolute certainty that history was synonymous with order. He was equally sure that a proper study of historical order would reveal its significance and its ultimate direction. Writing to Henry Cabot Lodge about his book *The Emancipation of Massachusetts*, he expressed his thoughts most succinctly:

> It is really not a history of Massachusetts but a meta-physical and philosophical inquiry as to the actions of the human mind in the progress of civilization; illustrated by the history of a small community isolated and allowed to work itself free. This is not an attempt to break down Puritans or to abuse the clergy, but to follow out the action of the human mind as we do of the human body. *I believe that we and they are subject to the same laws.*[12]

While the nature of the historical process was a symmetrical order, Adams believed that there were useful tools available for the historian to utilize in determining the major components of history. The most important was the application of a cause and effect technique to historical sequences. Every present effect had a previous cause. This was the stuff of history. An enormous chain linked all of the past to the total present. It had been this cause and effect chain "which for a fleeting mo-

[11] B. Adams, *The Law of Civilization and Decay*, 5.
[12] Quoted in Aaron, "Brooks Adams: The Unusable Man," *New England Quarterly*, Vol. XXI (March, 1948), 7. Italics are mine.

ment made the Iberian peninsula a centre of commercial exchanges."[13] The fall of Rome, the discovery of precious metals, and the Protestant Reformation were all links and could only be explained and understood by comprehending the links that preceded and those that followed.

Often the historian must consider the use of intuition or instinct by those individuals or nations which he is studying. Unconsciously, governments or races or institutions may enter into some undertaking without fully realizing why they are doing so. They react in obedience to an instinct or urge which has itself been impelled by natural law. A court may strike down a law on the basis of an intuitive feeling that the law is inimical to the numerical majority. A nation may go to war on some trifling pretext, when in reality it may have been guided by an unconscious instinct that its very life was at stake. When the historian encounters a situation in which he can perceive no visible cause and effect sequence, he should be alert to intuition and unconscious instinct as possible guides.

Adams firmly contended that the historian must never underrate the impact of the geographical environment on history. Here was another indispensable tool. Indeed, he concluded that "geographical conditions have exercised a great, possibly a preponderating, influence over man's destiny."[14] The failure of Greece to reach the imperial destiny that Periclean Athens had seemed to promise was almost directly attributable to her physical conformation. All areas of history were either favorably or adversely affected by the geographical environment, and no respectable historian could pursue the study of history without a thorough knowledge of geography.

Brooks Adams was consistent in his admonishments to historians about the necessary tools or insights they needed to possess. However, as a practicing historian, he, himself, has

[13] B. Adams, *The New Empire*, 90.
[14] *Ibid.*, iii.

left few clues to the amount of professional scholarship that he used when writing history. In fact, if judgments are to be rendered upon the soundness of his historicism, they must be based on scanty evidence. What evidence is available would seem to indicate that Brooks, unlike his older brother Henry, had most of the methodological vices usually found in the amateur. A credulousness, a distaste for documentation, an uncritical reliance on contemporary accounts, and a proneness to assume a theory as true before adequate proof was provided were all evidences of his failure to comprehend the use of the scientific method or to evaluate the responsibilities of the historian to his reading public. This is not to assume that his work was without merit, but the validity of his assumptions concerning the meaning of history must always be considered against this background of an unprofessional approach.

His credulity is perhaps best illustrated in his introduction to *The Emancipation of Massachusetts,* which purports to examine the trials of Moses and to draw a parallel between the leader of the Israelite exodus from Egypt and the leadership of the Puritan clergy in colonial New England. Much criticism has been leveled at this rather forced analogy, but what is equally significant is Adams' complete acceptance of the Biblical record as "good and trustworthy history."[15] In light of the scholarly reappraisals engendered by the higher criticism this is a most remarkable statement, particularly coming from one who was well known for his antifundamentalist views. The desire to substantiate a thesis at the expense of sound research technique smacks more of the propagandist than the historian.

[15] B. Adams, *The Emancipation,* 49. The *Nation,* in its review, commented that the book was "filled with tiresome rage against the Puritan clergy as a class." Furthermore, observed the reviewer, the reader is left "in utter darkness as to the object of the entire volume." It was then pointedly suggested that Adams showed more of the talent of the novelist than of the historian. Anonymous, review of *The Emancipation of Massachusetts* by Brooks Adams, *Nation,* Vol. XLIV (March 3, 1887), 189–90.

A similar amateurish characteristic is revealed in Adams' failure to check the accuracy and authenticity of his informational sources. If he found data that fitted his general plan, he used it and counted his sources trustworthy. Conversely, if statistics were uncovered which contradicted a cherished theory, the sources were denounced as faulty. Such manipulations are frequently encountered in his essay on the suppression of the monasteries during the English reformation. Adams depended largely on the dispatches of foreign ambassadors and observers in England, claiming that the reports of such agents had to be accurate because there were no newspapers. This is certainly an irrational dogmatism, in which the modern mind attempts to understand the spirit of the sixteenth century on twentieth-century terms. Moreover, he rejects the contemporary accounts of Englishmen, casually adjudging them to be distorted by prejudice because "the opinions of Englishmen are of no great value."[16] What is exposited by this observation is not the inherent prejudices of Englishmen but the Anglophobia of Brooks Adams.

In all fairness it must be admitted that Adams made no pretense at being an impartial historian. Impartiality to him meant an unwillingness to generalize and to search for a synthesis. He deplored the impact of German historiography on the writing of history, terming it a "dismal monster."[17] Ranke and his disciples had reduced history to a profession of dullness; Brooks Adams preferred the chronicles of Froissart or the style and theorizing of Edward Gibbon, for at least they took a stand on the issues about which they wrote. He wrote eloquently to William James that impartial history was not only impossible but undesirable. If the historian was convinced of his own correctness, then he should not allow his vision to be-

[16] B. Adams, *The Law of Civilization and Decay*, 180.
[17] B. Adams, "Collective Thinking in America," *Yale Review*, Vol. VIII (April, 1919), 623–24.

come fogged by disturbing facts. It was history that must be in error, not the historian. It was this basic trait that separated Adams from the ranks of professional historians and led him to commit time and time again what was his most serious offense against the historical method—namely, the tendency to assume the truth of an hypothesis before submitting it to the test of facts.

All of Adams' work reflects this dogmatic characteristic. No page seems to be complete without the statement of at least one unproved generalization. One example of this was his assertion that ". . . all servile revolts must be dealt with by physical force." There is no explanation of terms nor a qualification that most such revolts have been dealt with by force—only a bald dogmatism that they must, because of some undefined compulsion, be so repelled. On matters of race he was similarly inflexible: "Most of the modern Latin races seem to have inherited . . . the rigidity of the Roman mind."[18] He cites the French Revolution as typifying this rigidity but makes no mention of the Italians, who have been able to adapt to all types of circumstances. He pontificates that "one of the first signs of advancing civilization is the fall in the value of women in men's eyes."[19] It made no difference that most evidence points to an opposite conclusion. For Adams had made up his mind before all of the facts were available.

All critics of Adams and his methods have observed this particular deficiency. J. T. Shotwell was appalled by such spurious history as that which attributed the fall of the Carolingian empire to the woolen trade, and he urged Adams to "transform his essay into a real history, embodying not merely those facts which fit into his theory, but also the modifications and exceptions." A. M. Wergeland called the Adams method literally antihistorical, while Clive Day maintained that the assumptions

[18] B. Adams, *The Theory of Social Revolutions*, 29.
[19] B. Adams, *The Law of Civilization and Decay*, 297.

were not confined to theories alone but were also applicable to straight factual evidence. Moreover, stated Day, "He always omits facts which tend to disprove his hypothesis." Even D. A. Wasson, who compared *The Emancipation of Massachusetts* to the lifting of a fog from ancient landscapes, was also forced to admit the methodological deficiencies of the author.[20]

In summary, Brooks Adams felt that the nature of history was order and that the order so discovered was as much subject to historical laws as the forces of nature. Moreover, he believed that most professional historians lacked some of the essential instruments for a proper study of history. However, despite the insight of many of his observations, his own conclusions are open to suspicion because of his failure to employ at all times the correct research methods. This should not prejudice an evaluation of his findings, but they were not the findings of a completely impartial investigator. What was perhaps more important than his concept of the nature of history and the historical method were those forces which shaped the direction of his thought. In the final analysis his contribution to American historiography was founded on almost intuitive insights into religion, economics, and Darwinism, the three factors which conditioned his search for a law of history.

RELIGION WITHOUT SUPERNATURALISM

Brooks Adams considered religion as an extremely significant manifestation of man's fear of the unknown. But it was nothing more than that. Religion and the churches were institutions which had been created by man, not God. He did

[20] James T. Shotwell, Review of *The New Empire* by Brooks Adams, *Political Science Quarterly*, Vol. XVIII (December, 1903), 692–93; A. M. Wergeland, Review of *The New Empire* by Brooks Adams, *Dial*, Vol. XXXVI (January 1, 1904), 13–15; Clive Day, Review of *The New Empire* by Brooks Adams, *Yale Review*, Vol. XI (February, 1903), 421–23; D. A. Wasson, Review of *The Emancipation of Massachusetts* by Brooks Adams, *Atlantic Monthly*, Vol. LIX (February, 1887), 252–57.

not deny God; he simply did not believe that a Creator intervened or interfered in human affairs. The historian need not be concerned with the philosophical problems suggested by religion. There was no evidence, either of a positive or negative type, of the actions of a Divine Being in this world; and, since the historian should only be interested in strictly terrestrial activity, his research should eliminate the supernatural. Furthermore, he must regard religion as the expression of human forces. Certainly, he must recognize its power and attempt to ascertain its influence on the flow of history, but he must not confuse the natural and the mundane with the divine.

Adams was not breaking new ground when he claimed that the worship of an unseen power was in reality a reflection of man's inability to cope with his environment. Students of anthropology and comparative religion had long been aware that there was, indeed, a direct connection. But Adams was one of the first to suggest that this human incompetence was the only motivating factor behind religion. It was this fear which explained the development of a priestly caste whose function in society was to mollify and appease the angry deities. To keep themselves entrenched in power, the priests were forced to demonstrate their unique status through the miracle. It was the use of the supernatural that kept them in business. The German barbarians of the fourth century offered an excellent example:

> The Germans in the fourth century were a very simple race, who comprehended little of natural laws, and who therefore referred phenomena they did not understand to supernatural intervention. This intervention could only be controlled by priests, and thus the invasions caused a rapid rise in the influence of the sacred class. The power of every ecclesiastical organization has always rested on the miracle, and the clergy have always proved their divine commission as did Elijah.[21]

[21] B. Adams, *The Law of Civilization and Decay,* 54.

Adams contended that once such a special class had been created it became a vested interest and sought to maintain itself by assuming exclusive control over the relationships between God and man. Thus, the Church was born and because of its intrinsic character was soon identified as a conservative institution, determined to resist the forces of change, to identify itself with the political rulers, and to maintain a kind of splendid isolation from the masses. Doctrine was not only mysterious; it was also sacred, "and no believer in an inspired church could tolerate having her canons examined as we should examine human laws."[22] These basic ideas concerning the nature of religion were, Adams believed, some of the major keys to the understanding of history and the movement of society. The dark views about the Puritans found in *The Emancipation of Massachusetts* were never altered.

Despite their adherence to the *status quo*, the forces of organized religion were compelled to make adjustments as increasing civilization augmented human knowledge. In *The Law of Civilization and Decay* Brooks Adams traced this evolution, always pointing to the fact that although the forms became more rational, the substance remained unchanged. The relic worship and monasticism of the Middle Ages were more advanced forms than were primitive fetish worship and nature myths. Yet, the idea imbedded in each was identical: to surround the unknown with mystery and to isolate that class which had been given special dominion over the secrets of God. To Adams that age in which religion exercised power over the entire culture of the race was one of imagination, and it is largely the admiration he so obviously held for such eras that betrays a peculiar religiosity—a sentiment he would have probably denied.

Brooks Adams, like Henry, was impressed with the beauty and splendor of that lost time when the cathedral was the purest

22 B. Adams, *The New Empire*, xxii.

expression of human art. He could not help but feel a deep nostalgia for that period "when the imagination glowed with all the passion of religious enthusiasm" and when art was not a slave of commerce but instead was "an inspired language in which they communed with God."[23] Sacred architecture told the story of the rise of the imagination far better than anything else, and the bricks of Chartres were a symbolic poetry that transcended words. Adams looked back to the medieval period as a time when man had not been cheapened by the lust for money and material advantage. It made no difference that the religious framework rested on a fallacious foundation. Despite the fact that religion was grounded in fear and that the power of priests stemmed from exploiting that fear, the Middle Ages were still the best from both an artistic and moral viewpoint that man had been able to produce. Here in the twelfth and the thirteenth centuries Adams found beauty, security, and a serenity of mind that had not been available after the forces of economy had taken over. In words which were as rare as they were self-revealing, Brooks Adams expressed his sense of lost kinship with a forgotten God:

... but it might help man to know himself and hark back to God. For after all man knows mighty little, and some day may learn enough of his own ignorance to fall down again and pray. Not that I care. Only, if such is God's will, and Fate and Evolution— let there be God![24]

The termination of the age of imagination came when the priest and the soldier were trampled down by the more impersonal forces of economic competition. It was this point to which the social movement of history had been proceeding. In fact, Christianity had from the beginning carried within

[23] B. Adams, *The Law of Civilization and Decay*, 306.
[24] B. Adams, "Introduction," to H. Adams, *Degradation*, 99.

itself the seeds of its own destruction. To Adams this was demonstrated by the monetary value which came to be attached to the miracle. By allowing this to occur, he reasoned, the Church had made itself a party to the most degrading and degenerating of practices. The imagination cannot withstand the influences of an ever increasing materialism, and the Middle Age "though superficially imaginative, was fundamentally materialistic, as the history of the Crusades showed."[25]

Indeed it was the experience of the Crusades that prepared the way for the complete eradication of the medieval spirit that came with the Reformation. The great stimulus to trade and its resultant urbanization and increase in wealth were the major factors in replacing the priest with the merchant and in causing the miracle to be abandoned for the traditional thirty pieces of silver. Brooks Adams lamented the fact that "as wealth accumulated, and the economic type began to supplant the ecstatic, a different policy came to prevail." This different policy was accurately reflected in Church affairs by the middle of the twelfth century. The failure of St. Louis to repossess Palestine marked the beginning of the end, for his failure was more than a military one. It meant that "the idealist had begun to flag in the struggle for life."[26]

The disintegration reached its climax in that controversial series of events in the sixteenth century known as the Protestant Reformation. For Adams there were no unsolved problems concerning the deeds of Martin Luther and John Calvin. The Protestant leaders were simply the means through which the new forces of wealth found expression. The economic man would no longer tolerate the religious beliefs of his forebears; and the mighty upheaval of the Reformation was therefore, "but the supreme effort of the race to tear itself from the toils of a

[25] B. Adams, *The Emancipation of Massachusetts*, 116.
[26] B. Adams, *The Law of Civilization and Decay*, 125, 99.

hierarchy whose life hung upon its success in forcing the children to worship the myths of their ancestral religion."[27] The confiscation of monastic and other church lands especially in England, the failure of the Inquisition, and the support given by the new churches to the capitalistic economic policy of the state all, according to Adams, demonstrated conclusively the economic character of the Reformation. The Protestant convulsion then, to Adams, was not a rededication to forgotten religious principles but rather the final destruction of the core of original Christianity by the modern spirit of acquisitive capitalism. The priest had been dethroned; St. Bernard had been exchanged for Jakob Fugger. Religion ceased to occupy a role of paramount importance on the stage of history. Man would now find his motivations not in the miracle but in the florin.

Toward the end of his life Adams visited a Benedictine monastery and was once more caught up with the feeling that the solaces of medieval Christianity were the best the world had offered a suffering mankind. But the noise and confusion of a prosperity-mad America prevented him from staying in the quiet and loneliness of the monastery chapel. He told his friend Leonard Sargent that the world offered no relief. Tormentedly, he questioned, "Is there any spot on the top of this earth where a man like me could go and end his days in peace."[28] He knew in his heart the answer to his question. There was no safe place. For Brooks Adams history proved religion a fraud, for it had surrendered its once august position to economic determinism and evolution. What was even more tragic was the fact that there was nothing that could have been done to prevent it. History was determined by impersonal forces, and religion had been but a brief phase in the never ending movement of society toward death and decay.

[27] B. Adams, *The Emancipation of Massachusetts*, 172.
[28] Leonard Sargent, "An Adams in a Monastery," *Commonweal*, Vol. XIII (December 10, 1930), 156.

THE ECONOMIC DETERMINANT

The desire to acquire both money and property had largely determined the course of history since the Reformation. This was a basic premise in the historical philosophy of Brooks Adams. Competition for these things had been the driving force of civilization; it had been the motivating factor behind the great achievements in science and technology. It had also been the reason for the myriad wars which stained the story of modern man, for, in essence, war was simply "the most potent engine of economic competition."[29] Nor was there much hope that war would cease to be employed, since "war persists because civilization is always in movement."[30] The historian who wished to understand history had to recognize the economic drive. Just as fear had been the reason for the growth of religion, so greed was the motive in determining the rise of capitalism. If the historian took into account the twin impulses of greed and fear, and made them the dominant themes of human nature, then his history would rest on a solid base.

As already noted, the period from the Crusades to the Reformation had witnessed the life-and-death struggle between the instincts of fear and greed. The story of the growth of the Venetian state typified what was to occur throughout the rest of the earth. Venice became the greatest trading center in the civilized world, because the Venetians were more calculating and unscrupulous than their neighbors and because they lacked the imagination "which made the Northern peoples subservient to the miracle-worker." It was the Venetians who were responsible for spreading the commercial instinct until it had succeeded in penetrating the farthest reaches of the globe. It was no accident that the first gold coins were minted in Italy in

[29] B. Adams, *The Emancipation of Massachusetts*, 161.
[30] B. Adams, "Reciprocity or the Alternative," *Atlantic Monthly*, Vol. LXXXVIII (August, 1901), 145.

1252, for with the commercial supremacy of Venice, money became the new talisman and the trademark of an economic society.[31]

In addition, wealth had more than a symbolic value. Adams observed that wealth was the usual weapon of a monied society. What such a society lacked in imagination it compensated in money. The soldier who could no longer be bought with promises of salvation or relics could now be purchased with metals. Money was as surely the weapon of the capitalist as the sword had been the weapon of the medieval knight. As the supply of precious metals increased, so did the power of its capitalistic master grow in a direct ratio. It was inescapable, therefore, to conclude, thought Adams, that the introduction of currency had enormously accelerated social movement. The tremendous advances in material progress which had taken place since 1500 were proof of this. Another important result caused by the new emphasis on wealth was the transmutation of physical force into money. Whereas the basis of secular society in the early Middle Ages had been individual strength, the stress which modern society laid on money had made individual strength and courage obsolete.

Perhaps most important were the alterations in traditional concepts of justice and the role of courts that have been occasioned by the triumph of capitalistic economy. In previous ages the relationship between sovereign and subject had "been based either upon consent and mutual obligation, or upon submission to divine command."[32] In both cases there was the recognition of a responsibility residing on both parties. Adams contended that only in the master-slave relationship was there implied the idea that sovereign power was vested in an unaccountable superior. But the modern capitalist, claimed Adams, had succeeded in usurping the traditional relationship and in making

---

[31] B. Adams, *The Law of Civilization and Decay*, 4, 106–107.
[32] B. Adams, *The Theory of Social Revolutions*, 14.

himself a master in reference to his fellow citizens. He had accomplished this by influencing court systems as well as court personnel.

Brooks Adams deduced that the courts had forever been responsive to financial influences. And, furthermore, courts had always acted as the bulwarks of conservatism and as sturdy defenders of the *status quo*. It was a relatively simple matter, then, for capitalism to gain control of judicial systems. It was here that infiltration first began, and it was only after the courts were firmly held that attempts were made to influence executive and legislative branches. It was the courts who began to enforce with all of the hallowed traditions of the law the concept that the capitalist was somehow outside the normal legal restraints imposed by both custom and statute. Over a period of years enough decisions had been rendered to provide the new master with a halo of righteousness and to cloak his activities with the sacred vestments of judicial approval. Before these powerful combinations average citizens were helpless, for in their ignorance they did not realize that there was nothing sacred about the law or the men who interpreted it. They did not see that "law is merely the expression of the will of the strongest for the time being."[33]

Judicial bodies were not the only agencies which had been manipulated by capital and the greed for wealth. All history had to a greater or lesser extent felt the influence of this powerful economic factor. True, economic determinism could be most emphatically applied to the historical scene after 1500, but its impact could be detected in most events prior to that time. The development of the family in preliterary times from a group organized basically for the purposes of self-defense to a community of business interests was an example. The fact that in this new relationship the bonds of marriage assumed the form of a contract was further proof of the financial character

[33] B. Adams, *The Law of Civilization and Decay*, 137.

of the institution. Nor was the economic determinant confined to private groups. The decline of both Greece and Rome was directly attributable to similar factors.

The rapid disintegration of the political power of ancient Hellas after the Peloponnesian War has always been a phenomenon pondered by historians. The rapid rise to hegemony over the civilized world of Macedon under Philip and then Alexander has also been studied as one of those unexpected events which constantly plague the student who desires to see some order in the movement of history. For Brooks Adams these eternal riddles were not insoluble. Rather, they were confirmations of the power which metals had exercised on imperial and national growth. Alexander was able to conquer because Macedon "possessed richer mines than Attica."[34] The fall of the Roman Empire in the West and the maintenance of the Empire in the East at Constantinople were likewise the results of powerful economic forces, themselves largely the products of the drive for precious metals. Adams thought that surely he had suggested the only true interpretation of these hitherto inexplicable events.

With complete assurance in the validity of his presuppositions, Adams confidently applied the same formulas to situations in American history. Certainly, his essential concept of the nature of his country's history was economically determined, and all of his evaluations betrayed an economic base. Often these judgments seemed to be carried to rather extreme lengths. A typical and highly interesting example was his interpretation of the effect of the American Civil War upon England and English diplomacy. Adams attributed the British refusal to ally itself with the South to the precarious social equilibrium present in English society. The drive to extend the franchise, he claimed, was intimately connected with the restriction of extension of slavery in the United States. His reasoning ran thus:

[34] B. Adams, *The New Empire*, 36.

Hitherto, speaking broadly, the landed gentry had predominated, but, if the franchise were to be extended widely, none could tell whither power might migrate. Certainly, it would not remain with those who had enjoyed it. Therefore the aristocracy assuming that if the South should prevail the enfranchisement of the proletariat might be indefinitely postponed, the proletariat accepting it as axiom that their fortunes were bound up with the fortunes of the North.[35]

Of especial significance is the emphasis that Adams placed upon the class struggle as a determinant affecting national policy. He was almost purely Marxian in reaching the tenuous conclusion that the economic awareness of the proletariat prevented the gentry from sending arms and men to the beleaguered Confederacy.

World War I was the prime example, Adams believed, of the violent effects of economic competition. He disagreed most thoroughly with the Treaty of Versailles, feeling it to be too soft. He reasoned that since an economic war "is the fiercest and most pitiless of all wars . . . a lasting peace in competition implies either the extermination or enslavement of the vanquished." Because the Paris peace conference had imposed terms which would ultimately allow a return of Germany to economic competition, Brooks Adams predicted with unerring insight that "there must be a still more bitter struggle within a generation."[36] One may dispute the basis of his economic rationale, but the accuracy of his prophecy was proved by Hitler in 1939.

Economic factors were important forces in shaping the historical thought of Adams and in directing his search for a law. Yet, these factors were closely interwoven with another influence, the application of Darwinism to the historical process.

[35] B. Adams, "The Seizure of the Laird Rams," *Proceedings, Massachusetts Historical Society*, Vol. XLV (December, 1911), 327.
[36] "Introduction," to H. Adams, *Degradation*, 116–17.

It is often difficult to separate Adams' economic determinism from his fondness for the evolutionary theory. Indeed, they were probably intermingled in his own mind. But it is undeniably true that in his attempt to establish a scientific historical law, Brooks Adams embraced wholeheartedly the doctrines of Charles Darwin.

DARWINISM UNLIMITED

Brooks Adams never entertained more than the most momentary doubt that the principles given voice in *The Origin of Species* had special applicability to the study of history. When it came to finding the great motivating force which had impelled mankind on its trek through time, one needed to look no further than the Darwin-derived hypotheses of natural selection and the survival of the fittest. The historian's task was consequently made infinitely more simple. He did not have to ask why history moved as it did; he had only to chart the direction of the movement and to predict where future movement might lead. Nor was Darwinism some esoteric theory beyond the mental reach of the average historian; it was something visible in the natural process, if only the individual was willing to see it.

The use of evolutionary theory was particularly appropriate for the student who wished to observe the actions of nations and men scientifically. Adams maintained that abstract moral principles were poor standards for such a person to use when investigating customs and institutions. Life was a struggle for survival—a fact which was clearly evident after even the most cursory examination of the animal kingdom.[37] There was no reason to believe that the same principle did not apply to men. In fact, all of human history was a testament to the idea that

[37] B. Adams, *The New Empire*, xxiv; B. Adams, *The Emancipation of Massachusetts*, 298.

the laws of nature embraced all living things. The man who would survive to perpetuate his type was the one who best obeyed nature's inexorable demands. The one quality upon which nature most insisted was the capacity for men "to exert their energy through such channels as . . . may open from age to age."[38] It could be assumed as axiomatic, according to Adams, that men are capable of obtaining a livelihood under the conditions to which they are born. Furthermore, it must also be assumed that men have the flexibility to adapt themselves to changing natural conditions, so that existence may continue. "Hence, human customs, laws, and empires probably owe their rise and fall to the exigencies of that competition for food."[39] Natural selection was eternally in operation.

Nothing was more obvious to Brooks Adams than the fact that the weak perished and the strong survived. "Nature abhors the weak."[40] She was constantly developing new types to replace the older ones by imposing new conditions which required adjustment and adaptation. When any given type, dominant or not, failed to respond to the challenge, it was almost immediately superseded by a younger and more flexible type. He calculated that the replacement process of a specific type consumed about three generations, citing the rise to prominence of the moneylender after 1815 as a conspicuous example. The time it took to refurbish an entire civilization might well take considerably longer. An entire race which proved itself inadequate to meet the constantly altering demands of existence would be replaced in six centuries. Adams claimed that it was self-evident that the new types, individually and collectively, so produced would be strongest in those skills and attitudes in which their predecessors had been weakest. Consequently,

---

[38] B. Adams, "The New Industrial Revolution," *Atlantic Monthly*, Vol. LXXXVII (February, 1901), 165.
[39] B. Adams, "England's Decadence in the West Indies," *Forum*, Vol. XXVII (June, 1899), 464.
[40] B. Adams, *The New Empire*, 196.

there should be no difficulty in determining at any particular period what class has been the most recently formed. That class which owns the property, possesses political power, and has the most influence on legislation is the obvious selection. Dominant classes were bred to fit a special emergency. The danger lies in their refusal to perceive that with the passing of a crisis they may be unable to adapt themselves to change, in order that they may also survive future crises which are sure to occur.

"Competition," said Brooks Adams, "is the law of the flesh, and in a contest between the flesh and the spirit, in the end the flesh must prevail."[41] It was competition which had produced civilization. Every living organism "from the humblest peasant to the mightiest empire is waging a ceaseless and pitiless struggle for existence in which the unfit perish."[42] The stronger had always exterminated the weaker, and the strength of the flesh (arms and money) had proved more fit than the strength of the spirit (philosophy and religion). The law of evolution applied to the development of mind as well as the physical organism, and in the cutthroat competition of the world it was the rougher intellect which had survived. The failure of the Church in England to defend successfully the depredations against its property perpetrated by Henry VIII and Thomas Cromwell was illustrative of the triumph of the rough but hardy over the cultivated but weak. Indeed, it was one of Adams' more pessimistic pronouncements that human society tended to deteriorate rather than to progress, if one took for his measuring stick the human capacity for refinement. The last stronghold of the aesthetic, the fine arts, had succumbed to the strictures of competition. The impotency of man in the face of this irreversible process was nowhere more clearly visible than in the social upheavals called revolutions.

---

[41] "Introduction," to H. Adams, *Degradation*, 85.
[42] B. Adams, "Economic Conditions for Future Defense," *Atlantic Monthly*, Vol. XCII (November, 1903), 632.

Adams succinctly summarized his thoughts on revolutions when he said the following:

> Human society is a living organism, working mechanically, like any other organism. It has members, a circulation, a nervous system and a sort of skin or envelope, consisting of its laws and institutions. This skin, or envelope, however, does not expand automatically, as it would had Providence intended humanity to be peaceful, but is only fitted to new conditions by those painful and conscious efforts which we call revolutions.[43]

Despite the triteness of the analogy, Adams has painted a graphic picture, and one which carries more of the ring of truth than do many of his other observations. Put simply, he has pointed to that problem in history where Darwinist principles seem to have special significance. When the movement of history was so rapid that men could not adapt themselves to it, revolutions often occurred. The great upheaval of France in 1789 was a classic example.

Brooks Adams believed that not only was the French Revolution the most spectacular of revolutionary convulsions but also that it provided an especially instructive object lesson. This "annihilation of a rigid organism . . . throws into terrible relief the process by which an intellectually inflexible race may convert the courts of law . . . into the most awful engine of destruction."[44] The fall of the French monarchy took place not because of its oppression, but because it represented a medieval anachronism which failed to meet the challenges of a more modern time. Adams does not support the thesis that the French people in 1789 were thirsting after abstract ideals. What they wanted was "an administrative system which would put them on an

[43] B. Adams, "The Collapse of Capitalistic Government," *Atlantic Monthly*, Vol. CXI (April, 1913), 433. A similar statement may be found in B. Adams, *The Theory of Social Revolutions*, 132.

[44] B. Adams, *The Theory of Social Revolutions*, 135.

economic equality with their neighbors."[45] The *ancien régime* was obliterated because it was exactly that—an ancient way of government. Had the monarchy under Louis XV and Louis XVI been willing to make itself more flexible, to organize itself to meet modern situations, and to appreciate the inevitability of change, Robespierre, Danton, and Marat would never have become symbols of terror.

After the immediate shockwaves had dissolved into the anarchy of the Terror, the work of natural selection began. The Revolutionary Tribunals, asserted Adams, served this purpose by killing out the archaic mind in France. Once this had been accomplished, these natural forces, in supreme irony, dispensed with the very agent whose work had accomplished the mission. Robespierre went to the guillotine because he, like the monarchy, had been unable to adapt. Both offered indisputable proof that only the fittest survived. After the Terror modern France made a less violent readjustment "on the basis of unification, simplification of administration, and equality before the law, first under the Directory, then under the Consulate, and finally under the Empire."[46] Napoleon was the new type which nature had provided to meet the crisis of the age.

The experience of France, Adams insisted, provided lessons which the United States could ill afford to neglect. What had happened to the French monarchy under Louis XVI might well become the fate of America under an increasingly anachronistic capitalistic system. "Prudence, therefore, would dictate the adoption of measures to minimize the likelihood of sudden shocks." Brooks Adams warned his countrymen that the process of natural selection worked inexorably and that "those who fail to keep the pace are discarded." The one precaution which could be taken in order to avert such a fate was a toughening and strengthening of the intellectual quality so that "our

45 B. Adams, *The New Empire*, 160.
46 B. Adams, *The Theory of Social Revolutions*, 200–201.

descendants may be prepared to meet any eventuality."[47] It was not only possible but also imperative that the young be trained to adaptability.

Throughout history the United States had demonstrated flexibility, especially in her leadership. Two noteworthy examples were George Washington and John Hay. The first president had shown a remarkable capacity to meet the challenges of the times and to prepare himself for future crises. Adams declared that although Washington had been a conservative, he had seen the necessity of being progressive enough to "raise the law to a power high enough to constrain all these thirteen refractory units."[48] He had been able to make the necessary adaptation from thinking in terms of Virginia to reasoning in terms of union. Such a transition, Adams asserted, had been an absolute requirement for survival. Likewise, John Hay, as secretary of state for William McKinley and then Theodore Roosevelt, had illustrated a similar ability to realize the directions which history was taking. Moreover, Hay had the courage to act on those suppositions. His work in persuading England to abrogate the Clayton-Bulwer Treaty was of the greatest importance in opening commercial exchanges in favor of the United States; and his most significant accomplishment, the creation of the "Open Door" in China, recognized the fact that the future of the Western world lay in developing the resources of the Orient. Adams reasoned that a man who had been able to do this much and in addition "could serve equally well Lincoln, Greeley, and T. Roosevelt had to be able to survive."[49]

If she wished to survive as a great power, America must continue to possess the type of leadership personified by George Washington and John Hay. She also had to retain that flexibility

[47] B. Adams, *The New Empire*, 210.
[48] B. Adams, *The Theory of Social Revolutions*, 9.
[49] B. Adams, "John Hay," *McClure's Magazine*, Vol. XIX (June, 1902), 182.

and willingness to change that had stood her in such good stead during the financial disaster of 1893. But Adams was not so sure that his native land would continue to have the flexibility required by the natural forces. It was this haunting doubt that led him to the camp of free silver in the great "battle of the standards" in 1896. The gold standard, he claimed, was striking at the root of the social system because of its rigidity. He also objected strenuously to the discrimination in railroad freight rates on a similar basis, claiming that by penalizing the weaker classes to an extreme, there was the danger of social revolution. America's only hope was to move ahead, constantly and alertly. Institutions and traditions must not be allowed to obstruct the path of destiny. Even the Constitution must not take on the character of a sacred charter which was not subject to change. Adams warned that in such an event change would come violently, as it had done in France in 1789, and all our beliefs would be roughly thrust aside. What Americans had always to remember was the simple fact that the great movements of history "are not determined by argument, but are determined by forces which override the volition of man."[50]

Brooks Adams was completely convinced that he had discovered the essential ingredients with which to compound a law for history. He had sure-footedly trod a path through the labyrinthine passages of the past by employing the insights of religion, economics, and evolution as guides. What he had discovered was not a light of hope for bewildered mankind, because Adams had seen only a process which led inevitably downward. But by acknowledging the laws which governed his behavior, a man could prolong the process of decay. This was what Adams urged upon his countrymen. In this sense Brooks Adams was as romantic as his brother Henry. Both be-

[50] B. Adams, "Spanish War and World Equilibrium," *Forum*, Vol. XXV (August, 1898), 651. The theme of what America had to do specifically in meeting the challenges of the time was spelled out by Adams in a series of essays. See B. Adams, *America's Economic Supremacy*.

lieved passionately in the dignity of man to remain human in a universe that knew no human values. The search which Brooks Adams made for a law to explain history was nothing less than the eternal quest for truth which all men, in their own way, must undertake. The law of civilization and decay which was distilled from the forces of religion, economics, and Darwinism was, in reality, the record of one such journey.

5.

The Searches Compared

THE SEARCHES CONDUCTED BY Henry and Brooks Adams for an historical law have one great similarity. Both were attempting to provide an absolute synthesis which would illuminate the goal or end toward which history was moving. While there are other points of correlation, this likeness in motivation would appear to be the most important. Each was evidently compelled to undertake such a task because of the necessity for making some kind of sense out of the confusions and uncertainties of the modern scientific and industrial world. The moorings to the past had been slashed by the gigantic changes which swept the nation after the Civil War; there was, in consequence, a deeply felt need to find some explanation, some reason why the old order had changed. In another sense the search for historical laws was something more than the satiation of curiosity; the quest was also a romantic personal search for certainty in a civilization in which the former sureties had been destroyed. The paths which each Adams pursued took different routes; yet on many occasions they intertwined and crossed each other. Just as two personalities are never quite alike, so the methods employed by two inquiring minds may appreciably differ, even though they are seeking the same things.

Ironically, each arrived at opposite conclusions about the nature of history. Henry declared that history was chaos, while Brooks maintained that history was synonymous with order. But the variance was not as wide as might be initially supposed, for the terms of reference employed by each were dissimilar. When Henry spoke of chaos, he was actually referring to the possibility of purposefulness in human life. Indeed, the very lack of meaning which he detected did itself constitute something of a pattern, although not one which held any comfort for mankind. The fact that the universe operated along certain set lines was a formula which would have been readily accepted by Henry. Conversely, Brooks took as a frame of reference the concept of society as an organism. He was not looking for a cosmic teleology; rather, he was interested in determining whether or not human society operated according to observable laws inherent in nature. Considered from this viewpoint, the apparent separation between the two statements does not seem to constitute an unbridgeable chasm. Henry would agree that the social organism had to conform to natural law; in fact, this was one of his major hypotheses. Brooks would concur that there was nothing in the history of human civilization to warrant a belief in the benevolence of the universe or of a divine guidance directing the affairs of man.

As practicing historians, there was a vast difference between the two men. Henry Adams was always the professional; Brooks Adams was consistently the amateur. Henry seldom allowed his philosophical prejudices and inclinations to color his historical evaluations, while every investigation undertaken by Brooks was prompted by some preconceived idea for which he sought historical substantiation. Henry Adams made a careful study of sources, weighed evidence in a precise and logical manner, and reached conclusions only after the facts had been arranged and analyzed. Brooks Adams was careless in his use of documentary materials, and often reached conclusions on the basis of a priori techniques rather than through more scientifically valid methods.

Although the Adamses followed opposing research techniques, they shared some viewpoints about the character of the historical process. Both minimized the impact of the individual upon the direction of history, and they were especially skeptical concerning the role of the hero. In this area Brooks was more extreme than Henry, the former believing that the individual personality was a complete and impotent pawn in the hands of a relentless fate. Henry was unwilling to go quite that far, but he, too, deplored the tendency of historians to render uncritical adulation to historical personalities. Both Adamses also held little brief for the professional historians of their day. The main deficiency to which they strenuously objected was the apparent unwillingness on the part of the academicians ever to arrive at any meaningful synthesis. Both Henry and Brooks deplored the German emphasis on reconstructing the past exactly as it was. History was of small value unless it contained some validity for contemporary society. In that sense each foreshadowed the relativism of the next generation.

In their search for laws the Adams brothers quite naturally encountered the dominant ideas of their time. Each had to deal with these notions in order to achieve an intellectual balance and clarity. Again there may be observed both similarity and dissimilarity in their reactions. These were the results of varying environmental and ideological variations. Individual temperament, as in all instances, was of no little significance in producing varying responses. By comparing the receptiveness of Henry and Brooks Adams toward four principal ideas, the relative position of each emerges with a sharper clarity. These four problems are: the validity and meaning of religious experience, the role of evolution in shaping history, the importance of economic factors as historical determinants, and the nature and direction of natural law.

Nowhere is the contrast between the transcendentalist and the materialist in American culture more vividly personified than in the manner in which Henry and Brooks Adams regarded religion. Perhaps it would be more proper to state that the attitudes of the Adamses illustrate the decay of the old faith and the acceptance of a new one. Both, of course, recognized that religious faith was of utmost consequence to anyone engaged in determining the meaning and ultimate goals of history. Therefore, each deemed it necessary to examine carefully the vitality and integrity of religious experience.

Neither Henry nor Brooks was able to give approval to religiously oriented historical writing. Especially was this true of Christian eschatology. But whereas Brooks summarily dismissed religion as a product of humanity's fear of the unknown, Henry saw in religion man's most sincere attempt to provide unity and order to life. Thus, Henry's disillusionment and final skepticism becomes much more poignant than Brooks' rejection of the divine. For Henry's final conclusion that religion is without historical foundation implies that mankind's highest aspirations have been laughable frauds. The tragedy is heightened by the fact that Henry, himself, has such an emotional drive to believe. One never quite feels the same sense of cosmic disaster when contemplating the attitude of Brooks. He is one of the new materialistic breed who has nothing to lose by abandoning the old faith; he may feel a sense of occasional loss, but he is never moved to the pathos his brother exhibited in *Mont-Saint-Michel and Chartres*. It is impossible to read this volume without being aware that the author is not only a historian recreating an era but is also, himself, emotionally involved in the spirit of the age.

In relation to their search for a law of history, both renounced previous explanations which had assumed divine guidance or intervention in human affairs; however, the essential point is that Henry did so reluctantly, and Brooks, without apparent misgiving. Henry Adams foreswore religion because of a habit of skepticism, but Brooks Adams discarded orthodoxy because he had discovered a new faith.

That new faith was the evolutionary doctrine enunciated by Charles Darwin. This was, probably, the most influential current in nineteenth-century thought. Its emphasis upon the inevitability of natural selection and the survival of the fittest were ideas to which Brooks Adams fully subscribed. Competition was the key which explained the behavior of all nature. Everything and everybody were engaged in a merciless struggle for existence, and the results of this struggle were what determined the character and direction of history. Henry Adams never accepted these tenets in the total fashion that his brother did. Conditioned by an ingrained skepticism, the elder Adams viewed with circumspection any theory which professed to be a complete answer. Moreover, Henry most violently objected to the implied suggestion of the evolutionists that the natural movement of history was progressive and upward. He, himself, saw exactly the opposite trend. His unwillingness to accept progressive evolution made him suspicious of utilizing its other tenets. Brooks, too, did not see progress in a spiritual sense in the evolutionary doctrine. To Brooks the idea that the fittest survived did not, of necessity, imply that the fittest were also the best. Rather, he inferred that those things which were the cheapest were the ones that were the fittest.

Evolution was vital to each of the Adamses in his search for a law. For Brooks it was to become the cornerstone of his philosophy when it was combined with economic determinism. Henry's repudiation of the progressive character of evolution was to lead him to the theory which he eventually adopted— namely, degeneration. It would be correct to assume that the reaction of the Adamses to the Darwinian ideas, so much debated and discussed during their lifetimes, was the crucial point in the formation of their laws for history.

The importance of economic factors in shaping history was becoming increasingly apparent in the latter years of the nineteenth and early ones of the twentieth centuries. Both Henry and Brooks Adams were alert to the new forces and aware of the manner in which they were transforming the nation. However, there was a basic difference in their responses. Henry was repelled by what he saw and Brooks was curiously attracted. Again, there can be noted the clash of the old and new Americas—Henry, perhaps unconsciously, was still devoted to Jeffersonian agrarianism; Brooks had never been under its spell. For him economic factors, coupled with Darwinism, became fundamental in interpreting historical phenomena. Man's desire to own property was the key to understanding the course of human history. In his stress upon the power of economics Brooks Adams reflected the Marxist influences of his own day, and he anticipated the economic determinist school of historians who would flourish in the United States for thirty years.

Henry Adams could never generate the enthusiasm for the economic in history that Brooks did. Indeed, there is little evidence that he gave it much consideration at all until requested to do so by Brooks, preparatory to the publication of the latter's *The Law of Civilization and Decay*. He was impressed with Brooks' theories and with their emphasis upon economic determinism. But he was not content to accept them as final in themselves. He insisted upon looking beyond their outward manifestations to their sources. In so doing his own research received a significant impulse. Henry saw the great economic movements of his time as symbols of energy—energy which was being wildly and recklessly dissipated. The economic factor in history, which Brooks tended to accept as absolute, was interpreted by Henry as providing unique insight into the operation of natural laws.

Henry and Brooks Adams could both argue, with equal justification, that their researches had led to the conclusion that history was as dependent upon natural law as any other element in the universe. Each also would eventually arrive at hypotheses which were alike in their pessimism concerning the future. Where one predicted a gradual degradation of energy, the other foresaw a series of events leading to decay. But the point at which they diverged was the scale on which they viewed the operation of natural law. Brooks Adams based his conclusions concerning the movement of history squarely on what could be observed in the biological record. He agreed that energy was being expended, but his only concern was its expenditure here on earth. Henry Adams adopted the more cosmic scale. For him, the entire universe needed to be examined before any deductions could be made concerning human history. Where Brooks depended almost solely on Darwinian biology for support, Henry looked to physics and astronomy as being equally vital. Thus, what the physicist had to say about the expenditure of energy in space had a direct bearing on the future direction of history.

In reality, therefore, the searches which the two brothers conducted for historical laws took each far afield from the ordinary paths of historical studies. Since neither preferred to look to God in the manner of St. Augustine or Bishop Bossuet, each had to look to some other absolute for proof. Brooks thought that he had found such a certainty in the application of biological science to history; Henry believed that the application of the laws of physics was the answer. Both appealed, therefore, to the absolutism of science. The cardinal mistake which each made was the unwarranted assumption that either biology or physics was infallible. Further scientific effort was to show that science was still all too ignorant concerning the workings both of the universe and of this humble planet earth.

6.

Henry *Adams: The Law*

FOUNDATIONS

THE ANNOUNCEMENT BY Henry Adams of a law which explained all historical movement was the result of a lifetime spent in studying history and meditating on its inner dynamics. The enunciation was neither as sudden nor as startling as it seemed. Adams, himself, was not completely aware that the formulation of such a law had been something toward which the nature of his historical work had been moving from the beginning. Critics who complain that the law of degeneration was a theory advocated by Adams on a sudden impulse after a momentary fascination with the new physics of Kelvin have not examined the total structure of Adams' philosophy. Many serious objections may be raised concerning the validity of the law in its applicability to actual historical situations; however, the suggestion that it was superficial and prompted only by the innate irascibility of its author is not prompted by the facts. There are enough statements made by Adams throughout his life to suggest a pattern which eventually produced a law for history.

Henry Adams first began to meditate seriously on the complexities of history when he acted as secretary to his ambassador father in London during the Civil War. The proximity of well-known diplomatic personnel, coupled with the precarious and vital mission to which his father had been entrusted, undoubtedly produced within the young Adams a heightened sense of history. Although he deplored what he considered the evil machinations of men like Palmerston, Lord Russell, and Gladstone, he was still intensely interested in the great drama in which they had leading parts. With the vigor and sureness of youth he was also confident that what appeared to be mere chance would someday be explained by science, believing that "every part of nature will be brought . . . within this law."[1] Moreover, he asserted that a similar set of laws would be discovered which governed both animate and inanimate nature. While this tone was decidedly optimistic and later pronouncements would evince a strong pessimism, the basic faith remained intact. The law which Adams finally espoused was certainly one that exuded little hope for the future, but it was a law which was firmly based on the idea he had professed as early as 1862. It was indeed an hypothesis which assumed an undergirding formula for the entire universe.

Another facet which was omnipresent was Adams' necessity for seeing unity in history. This drive for simplicity, for a single answer, was not unique. All human beings must in their own way make some intelligibility out of the multiplicity of experience. Since the reason operates in but a single dimension and is unable to view events either simultaneously or totally, the answers which the mind advances must of necessity be of a unitary nature. Despite its awareness, therefore, of the individual's lack of perspective, the reason has to arrive at an answer which will satisfy the requirements of orderly living. The historian, either consciously or unconsciously, performs a similar operation on history, no matter what technique or reconstruction he employs. Henry Adams was acutely aware of this historical task. Perhaps the impulse for unity and explanation was stronger in him than in others; but it was a compulsion which

[1] H. Adams to B. Adams, April 2, 1898, in Ford, *Letters*, II, 163.

never left him; it was the motivating force behind all of his historical scholarship. History and historians desperately needed to find the secret of unity.

As early as 1884, Adams had predicted to Francis Parkman that a new scientific law would be discovered which would antiquate previous theories. He was completely convinced that the time was near when "psychology, physiology, and history will join in proving man to have as fixed and necessary development as that of a tree."[2] It was unbelievable that man should be able to predict the movement of planets, plot the direction of ocean currents, yet know so little about himself. Most historians had utterly failed to provide the race with anything but mere antiquarianism, and those who made the attempt to link facts with ideas, like Buckle, were regarded as failures.[3] For decades English writers of history had written everything except what should have been written, believing that the field of "history, like everything else, might be a field of scraps, like the refuse about a Stratfordshire iron-furnace." Gibbon had begun such a cycle of nonsense when he had written about the fall of Rome without any understanding of the Roman contribution to the Western world.[4] American historians were not improving the situation. Like their English cousins, they failed to see that the forces which were behind the movements of history were far more important than the movements themselves.[5] But the times were bright with change; everything was being placed under the microscope of science. History had no choice

---

[2] Letter of December 21, 1884, in Cater, *Friends*, 134.

[3] H. Adams, *Education*, 221. Adams was particularly scathing in his reviews of E. A. Freeman's works, considering them to be typical of English shortcomings. Freeman "shows only limited capacity for critical combinations, and he has a true English contempt for novel theories." H. Adams, Review of *Historical Essays* by E. A. Freeman, *North American Review*, Vol. CXIV (January, 1872), 195.

[4] *Ibid.*, 221, 93.

[5] H. Adams, Review of *The Old Regime in Canada* by Francis Parkman, *North American Review*, Vol. CXX (January, 1875), 175.

but to do likewise. It was difficult for the impatient Adams to understand why historians were so reluctant to join the great search, when the need for law and synthesis was so painfully obvious in the history they wrote about.

Every period of history that he studied confirmed his opinion that all was chaos and that new explanations were needed. His perusal of the origins of medieval institutions, as a director of seminar research at Harvard, showed him only that he could give his students no answers. The professor of physics could describe physical forces, but the historian was helpless. No one had solved the riddle of the Middle Ages. If explanations and reasons were desired, the historian was incapable of helping. History was "a hundred years behind the experimental sciences" and "less instructive than Walter Scott or Alexander Dumas."[6] To study the thirteenth century and the philosophy of Thomas Aquinas was similarly frustrating. That age which was considered to be the most unified, the most logical of any in the history of Christendom was a mass of contradiction. Historians wrote volumes describing the society, philosophy, economy, art, and politics of the age; but none explained the symbolism of the Virgin who dominated the era. This, he thought, was inexcusable. Here was a great symbol of the unity of an age, and everybody ignored it.[7]

The same inadequacy could be detected in the writing of American history. The great war between the states had been as fantastic a blood-bath as the civilized world had witnessed. But what had caused it? History, which had been entrusted with rendering a decision, only debated and vacillated between scores of conflicting alternatives. Certainly, here was chaos gone rampant. No one ever labored more diligently than Henry Adams to penetrate the historical forces which operated during the Jeffersonian period, but when everything had been done,

[6] H. Adams, *Education*, 301, 306.
[7] H. Adams, *Mont-Saint-Michel*, 288–89, 420.

he decided that he had unmasked no forces. What had been accomplished was a mastery of the historical method, not history.[8] In addition the problem seemed to become more complex when one attempted to write contemporary history. If the nature of those forces which had been the impetus of the ancient and medieval past was still obscure, how much more secret were the dynamics of the present. To Adams the problem was crucial. With the world rushing at breakneck speed to an unknown destination, propelled by forces it did not understand, history had to have some answers. Modern man had to be told what he was doing and where he was going. History had to interpret both the past and present.

Adams was certain that historians had been pursuing misleading pathways in their efforts to discover a suitable approach to truth. He, himself, had followed traditional methods in studying the history of the United States, and he had come no closer than previous writers in disclosing the real motivations, the guiding forces which had been dominant. Historians were too obsessed with the multitudinous facts about the past. They forgot that all facts were senseless unless they revealed the secret of their formation. There was force present in history—a guiding, pervasive, dominating force. This was what had been ignored. If science had pushed back the frontiers of geology, biology, and physics by explaining phenomena in terms of energy, the historian should be able to do the same thing. Man was a part of nature; nature was directed by force. It followed, therefore, that man and the story of his activities were likewise subject to laws of force. What required determining was the nature of the force and a calculation of the direction in which it was proceeding.

It is important to remember that in the mind of Henry Adams the terms "force" and "unity" were nearly synonymous. One was not complete without the other. If unity or purpose existed

8 Ernest Samuels, *The Young Henry Adams*, 266.

in history, it existed only because there was a common unitary force which was its core. From the opposite angle of vision it could be said that if such a force could be proven, then the unity of history was an evident fact. Adams was quick to point out the inseparability of the two ideas and to note further that his assumption was a foundation for all philosophic systems and for all philosophies of history. "The direction of mind, as a single force of nature, has been constant since history began."[9] All great synthesizers had assumed unity as a force, and some had given it names. What Aquinas called God, Spinoza termed a "substance," and Kant, the "categorical imperative." The definitions made little difference; it was the presupposition that was important. The entire purpose of the quest of Henry Adams was to establish the validity of the assumption. He set forth the problem in the simplest of terms:

> Unity either is, or is not. . . . The attempt to bridge the chasm between multiplicity and unity is the oldest problem of philosophy, religion, and science, but the flimsiest bridge of all is the human concept, unless somewhere, within or beyond it, an energy not individual is hidden; and in that case the old question instantly reappears: What is that energy?[10]

By concluding that the force of history was an energy, even a mental energy, Adams limited the boundaries of potential explanations to the field of physics. The true historian must not only be scientific in method, but he must also be scientific in the explanations he presented. He must be like the mathematician with a slide rule; he must become the true scientist, deciding what it was he had to measure and what tools were required to perform the measurement. Until historians acknowledged this verity, they would be but amateurs in the world of science.

9 H. Adams, *Education*, 456.
10 H. Adams, *Mont-Saint-Michel*, 337.

It was the Chicago Exposition of 1893 that finally gave Adams a start toward the conclusion he would eventually reach. Here, typified by the dynamo, was the first actual expression of American unity. Just as the Virgin symbolized the unity of the medieval synthesis, so the dynamo represented the forces of modern civilization. The contemporary American placed as much absolute faith in electricity as his thirteenth-century predecessor had put in the power of Mary. Both posited the existence of an ultimate—an absolute substance which lay behind all of the attributes and outward appearances of things. Indeed, the existence of both made possible the existence of a law, for a law of history was only possible if an ultimate was a reality. Both the Virgin and the dynamo were articles of faith. There was no understanding of either. For the moment Adams was dismayed. He pondered the possibility that perhaps St. Bernard had been right all along in claiming that the only avenue to truth was faith, that it could not be approached through the intellect. However, his intense pride refused to admit incomprehensibility. The search continued; a new education at the age of fifty-five began. Its fruition was the law of degeneration.

One historian has perceived three essential levels of development in the progress of Henry Adams toward the construction of a scientific law of history.[11] The first stage came from his early conviction that history must be treated as a physical science—a conviction which stemmed from contacts with the new German emphasis upon method. The second stage was best represented by *A Letter to American Teachers of History*, in which he first applied the thermodynamic principles of Lord Kelvin to history. The third stage was visible in *The Rule of Phase Applied to History*, which represents his abdication as an historian and the abandonment of history to the mathematicians and physicists. However, the line dividing the second stage from the third is indistinct. The rule of phase essay does

[11] James Truslow Adams, *The Tempo of American Life*, 224-25.

not repudiate the conclusions reached through thermodynamics. Rather, it is a simple extension and application of the propositions exposited in his letter to teachers. Yet there is some merit in noting this stair-step development, for it is a fairly accurate record of Adams' intellectual evolution into the intricacies of science. Furthermore, it suggests a scientific orientation even before he had embraced physics as a new Moses destined to lead historians out of the wilderness.

There were five writers who were mainly responsible for this orientation: Auguste Comte, Sir Henry Buckle, Charles Darwin, Sir Charles Lyell, and Herbert Spencer. Adams readily admitted his indebtedness to Comte and Buckle.[12] The French positivist and the English historian demonstrated for him the reliability of using science as a satisfactory approach. Their conclusions about history were not nearly as important as the methods they employed and their insistence that science could be applied to the historical process. Darwin and Lyell were significant in a less positive manner. As previously mentioned, Adams thoroughly rejected the progressive idea inherent in evolutionary schemes, but his acquaintance with the efforts of Spencer to use the findings of men like Darwin and Lyell to explain the movements of society persuaded him to seek alternatives. Although Adams deplored the popularity of Spencer, his own efforts were similar to those of the author of *Social Statics*.[13] Thus, the influence which was exercised over his own deliberations by the aforementioned authors was more qualitative than quantitative. Henry Adams was but one of a large number who believed that society was an organism which could be dissected and explained in as scientific a fashion as any other organism.

Once the assumption had been made concerning the organic

[12] Robert A. Hume, *Henry Adams: Runaway Star*, 214; H. Adams, *Education*, 225.

[13] Roy F. Nichols, "The Dynamic Interpretation of History," *New England Quarterly*, Vol. VIII (June, 1935), 164–65.

nature of society, all that remained for the historian was to determine the force or forces which directed the life of the society. Modern technology had succeeded in making visible to all the existence of such forces. The time sequences of the evolutionary historian had been obliterated; the mind-impulse of the idealists had been shattered. What remained was the sequence of force. The examination of this sequence proved to Adams that man could never really know the composition of the forces; he might discover their destination, which Adams felt to be degeneration, but he was as helpless before them as he once had been before the power of religion. The physical laws that seemed to govern history were infinite and omnipotent.[14] Science produced the greatest irony of all. After promising hope, she disclosed a hopeless universe.

ENUNCIATION

The historical law announced by Henry Adams was based on two hypotheses of the new physics. One was Kelvin's second law of thermodynamics which, simply put, argued that energy was being dissipated rather than conserved and that the universe would culminate in an eternal lifelessness. The second was Willard Gibbs' rule of phase which stipulated the behavior of chemical components within a closed system or in an equilibrium.[15] Adams never fully comprehended the scientific background of either theory, and he was guilty of great oversimplification in his interpretations. This was especially true in the case of the latter theorem, for Gibbs' studies cast serious doubts on the validity of the second thermodynamic law—a fact which might easily have destroyed Adams' historical law.[16] However,

---

[14] H. Adams to B. Adams, March 4, 1900, in Ford, *Letters*, II, 271.

[15] The scientific explanations of these two ideas are far too complex and mathematical to be a proper part of this study. Such explanations and the degree of understanding which Adams had of them are thoroughly explored in William H. Jordy, *Henry Adams*, 166–72.

we are not concerned here with the accuracy of the scientific knowledge of Henry Adams or the scientific validity of the involved calculations. Rather, this is an attempt to evaluate only the Adams law insofar as it affected the development of historiography. What is important then is not what Kelvin and Gibbs construed their researches to be but what Henry Adams thought them to be and how he adapted them to the study of history.

The first step was to prove that history was an energy. Adams had already satisfied himself that it was a force. It had been this conclusion which had been the foundation for his belief in the possibility of discovering a law. But there was a subtle distinction to be made between force and energy. Force is a vague generalized abstraction that describes a motivating power; energy deals directly with the nature of the power. The steam engine and the dynamo both illustrate a principle of force, but their energy is quite different. One must be able to calculate the energy before one can predict the movement of force. The problem, therefore, was to determine the energetic nature and composition of the force of history.

It was obvious to the most casual observer "that the energy with which history had to deal could not be reduced directly to a mechanical or physico-chemical process."[17] However, neither could the casual observer deny the existence of an energy which permeated society. This social energy was as real as electricity. To deny the existence of such energy would be to deny one's own personal existence. Examples were plentiful, but in 1905 the best proof of social energy was the constant activity of Theodore Roosevelt, who "more than any other man living within the range of notoriety, showed the singular

---

[16] *Ibid.*, 167. Jordy has effectively explored the naïve assertation of J. T. Adams that "On the whole, perhaps no other American has been so well-fitted as he [Henry Adams] to make the effort to establish scientific law in history, if it is possible." J. T. Adams, *Tempo of American Life*, 216.

[17] H. Adams, "Letter," in *Degradation*, 142.

primitive quality that belongs to ultimate matter."[18] Roosevelt was social energy in its purest form. The historian was faced with the task of devising a method by which such energy could be measured and predicted. He could not apply the traditional yardsticks of the sciences. The essential point for students of history was to realize that social energy, although real, was unique and was governed by its own laws.

But this did not imply that the total energy was not subject to a universal regulation which governed the expenditure of any type of energy. For example, a railroad engine may be propelled down a track by different types of energy—steam, electricity, or gasoline. The laws governing the output of each energy are different; yet, the impact of each energy on the engine is the same. In other words, social energy is produced by its own set of laws but is still subject to a law which controls the dispensation of all energies. Since Adams accepted the idea that all energy was being dissipated, it followed that social energy was also irrecoverable and that history was subject to the same principle of degradation that seemed to dominate the energies of the physical world.

Historians had long ignored this harsh truth, nor did Adams feel that they had any present desire to consider seriously the principle of degradation. Faculties at universities were committed to a belief in the potentiality of raising mankind through education to a nobler life. They could hardly be expected to subscribe to a theory which negated their very *raison d'être*. Nor could religion accommodate itself to the new principle. It was as dedicated to a scheme of progress as was the evolutionist. It could not be expected to turn against itself. Even the solitary individual would discover it almost impossible to accept an idea which postulated his own destruction. Man was an egocentric being, and his instinct made him reject the proof. The ego would renounce degradation "though science should prove

[18] H. Adams, *Education*, 417.

twenty times over . . . that man is a thermodynamic mechanism."[19] If neither evolution, religion, or the individual thinker would accept the task of measuring degradation, then the job was left only to the historian or the physicist who could divorce himself from his own instincts. Henry Adams had little hope that his colleagues in the study of history would meet the challenge.

Henry Adams, himself, made some attempt at correlating history to the law of degradation, of estimating the amount of social energy which hitherto had been expended, and of calculating both the amount of energy remaining to humanity and the rate at which it was being discharged. His inspiration for such calculations came from the rule of phase which Willard Gibbs had demonstrated as having validity for elements within an equilibrium. What Adams did was to substitute within the Gibbs formula historical for chemical components. Whereas water might be the subject for investigation by the physicist who wished to observe it in varying stages of equilibrium, Adams selected man's thought to be considered "as a single substance passing through a series of historical phases."[20] The alterations which water undergoes are affected by the application of three determinant variables—pressure, temperature, and volume. Each of these variables exercises a decisive influence on the state of water when it is suspended in a state of equilibrium (e.g., a salt solution). Adams contended that a similar process may be observed by the historian. In place of pressure the historian must substitute attraction. This is the variable which gives history its forward movement; and the larger the mass (thought), the greater the force of attraction.[21] For the second variable, temperature, Adams would interpose acceleration. Just as water undergoes a drastic alteration when there is coin-

[19] H. Adams, "Letter," in *Degradation*, 226-27.
[20] H. Adams, "The Rule of Phase," in *Degradation*, 275.
[21] *Ibid.*, 274.

cidental application of pressure and temperature, so also must history undergo convulsion when the force of attraction and acceleration reach a certain point. The third important variable, volume, appears unchanged in the historical phase. The result is that the progress of thought may be calculated mathematically, just as the changes in water may be predetermined. Thought will behave in accordance with the rule of phase and increase in volume according to the law of inverse squares. If all of this were true, the task of the historian became quite simple. All he needed to do was to learn how to apply the formula within a framework of degradation. Indeed, there was no longer any real use for the historian. He must abandon his field to the physicist. "Sooner or later, every apparent exception, whether man or radium, tends to fall within the domain of physics."[22] The time had come for history; it had to yield.

APPLICATION

Examples and illustrations of the degradation thesis are to be found throughout the writings of Henry Adams. Many of his remarks which show the influence of a philosophy of degeneration were made before he had clearly formulated his views in the first decade of the twentieth century. This gives substance to the assertion that his eventual embracement of the degradation doctrine was not a spontaneous romance with the second law of thermodynamics, but a gradual growth to which Lord Kelvin only gave the finishing stroke. Too, Adams was by inheritance and inclination a pessimist, and a philosophy which confirmed his pessimism was attractive. His great antipathy to the claims of the Darwinians, as has already been noted, was more than an intellectual reaction. Optimism was not a part of his character, nor did he see much in the world's history to change his position.

[22] H. Adams, "Letter," in *Degradation*, 224-25.

The physical aspect of man's nature was offered as evidence in favor of degradation. Certain faculties, such as an instinctive color-sense, had been lost down the vast stretches of time.[23] Society might protest most vigorously that its senses had not been dulled through the years, but such protests did not lessen the validity of the claim. Modern man, far from being at the apex of a progressive evolution, was in fact "the most advanced type of physical decadence."[24] He was not at the top of the ladder but at the bottom. Human pride and human institutions prevented responsible members of society from making the admission; yet this same pride and these same sacrosanct institutions were themselves solid examples of the degeneracy in human energy and the decay that was apparent from every angle.

Social institutions by their very nature became entrenched and resistant to any idea which appeared to threaten their existence. However, any historical theory which would hold such institutions to be symbols of degeneration, rather than dynamic instruments of progress, had little likelihood of winning acceptance. Institutions had already won acceptance; otherwise, they would not be institutions. The church was the most powerful; the state stood next, followed by the institutions of property and labor. The fact that each refused to admit any theories not consistent with its own strength was in itself proof of degeneration. To point out that groups like the church and the state incorporated degenerative ideas in their own philosophies was useless. The church paid no heed, despite the evidence that the principal justification for religion was the assumption of human degradation, alleviated only by the pity of God. The state insisted on the need for the police power, in order to coerce its citizens into doing those things which an improving humanity would have performed automatically. To Henry Adams the simple existence of institutions, encrusted

[23] H. Adams, *Mont-Saint-Michel*, 151.
[24] H. Adams, "Letter," in *Degradation*, 162.

with the halos of tradition, was an ever present proof of human degradation which even the most optimistic of historians had not failed to notice.

Historians had always used the principle of degradation to some degree in writing history. The most outspoken prophets of progress often slipped into thermodynamic terminology. According to Adams, Macaulay talked about the depleted energies of Great Britain and Gibbon interpreted the barbarian invasions of the Roman Empire as an infusion of fresh fuel "flung on the burnt-out energies of empire."[25] It was natural for the scholar who had spent years in the study of history to think in such terms, for this was what he encountered. Surely, of all people the historian should be conscious of degeneration, as he had the best basis for comparison. One who had looked into the past but must live in the present cannot help but be conscious of the gradual debasement of society. Adams could see only descent in the path which led from the cathedral age in France to Boston. "Since then our ancestors have steadily declined until we have reached pretty near the bottom."[26] He wondered why the evident fact of degeneration was not apparent to the most amateur of historians. Why did history departments so vigorously maintain progressive evolution in the light of the facts? He answered his own question.

Professors of history were greatly dependent on maintaining the idea that thought was progressive. If they accepted the second thermodynamic law as being applicable to themselves, they were co-operating in their own destruction. "Of all possible theories, this is likely to prove the most fatal."[27] The historian

[25] *Ibid.*, 240–41.

[26] H. Adams to B. Adams, September 8, 1895, in Ford, *Letters*, II, 80. In commenting on the state of France and England, Adams said: "The British system, like the French, was in its last stage of decomposition. Never had the British mind shown itself so *decausu*—so unravelled, at sea, floundering in every sort of historical ship-wreck." H. Adams, *Education*, 193.

[27] H. Adams, "Letter," in *Degradation*, 195.

cannot possibly admit that his own work exists "only as a sporadic survival to illustrate for his colleagues the workings of their second law of thermodynamics."[28] Departments of history in the universities were anachronisms. They refused to correlate their researches with the departments of physics and mechanics from which they had so much to learn. Inertia had claimed the writer of history. He was a monument to the principle of degradation, a living testimonial to the failure of civilization to produce either a better man or a safer world.

To Henry Adams civilization had not led upward. It had been a constant movement downward, whose direction had been hidden from onlookers by technological advance which had been mistaken for progress. As early as 1883 he had concluded that the history of society, like water, pursued the line of weakest resistance.[29] All that technology had accomplished was an increase in the rate of acceleration with which society sought the lowest level. This seeming paradox was in reality no contradiction. It depended on the definition of civilization. If civilization was to be gauged by the number of physical improvements that had been made, then modern society had definitely shown progress. However, if civilization was defined as an increase in and refinement of human energies and ideals, there was obvious degeneration in contemporary culture. Indeed, the fact that man had made unprecedented strides in the use and expenditure of energy testified to the rapid exhaustion of his personal resources and his increasing dependence on natural reserves. To Adams modern man was not the equal of his more barbaric progenitors. Not only was he weaker physically and spiritually, he was also no wiser. He had unleashed forces which carried him along like the aimless driftwood in a raging river. He did not have the slightest idea where he was going. What was worse, he did not seem to care.

[28] *Ibid.*, 245.
[29] H. Adams to Samuel Jones Tilden, January 24, 1883, in Cater, *Friends,* 126.

Looking ahead, Henry Adams perceived that the modern world was racing toward a rendezvous with catastrophe. Economically, he foresaw an inevitable drift toward socialism, which was the cheapest of social systems. He agreed with his brother Brooks that the concentration of capital would bring the "Russian millenium of a centralized, despotic socialism."[30] This would mean the collapse of individualized human effort and further evidence to support the degradation thesis. The future of politics and culture was also most gloomy. Nothing would survive the depletion of energy. All human activity was seeking the lowest plane of existence. Man had tinkered with a loaded shell, and his adventures in science would eventually be his ruin. The next hundred years would witness an "ultimate, colossal, cosmic collapse."[31]

This was what the theory of degradation saw in the past, observed in the present, and forecast for the future. Civilization had been conceived in mystery; it would die in similar silence. The great irony was that civilization itself was a portent of decay. The concentration of social forces which it had produced had been the first harbinger of the final disaster. What was even more ironic was the fact that the passengers on this speeding vessel thought they were on a pleasure cruise, when in reality they were aboard a ship which would find no safe harbor and was doomed to become inert and lifeless on a sterile sea.

By applying the rule of phase to history, Adams attempted to calculate the speed with which society was moving toward its disastrous destination. He conceived of civilization or thought as passing through a series of stages, much in the same manner as water undergoes a set of phases when it is acted upon by pressure, temperature, and volume. The historical pressure

---

[30] H. Adams to W. C. Ford, December 19, 1898, in Ford, *Letters*, II, 197; H. Adams to B. Adams, October 31, 1899, in *ibid.*, 246.

[31] H. Adams to B. Adams, August 10, 1902, in Cater, *Friends*, 529.

of attraction, acceleration, and volume had produced for civilization four stages, of which only three were apparent to the historian. They were: the age of instinct, about which little could be learned because of the lack of much documentary or archaeological evidence; the age of religion, which stretched from the beginnings of recorded history to 1660 (during this period man was forced to rely on the supernatural for aid against the vicissitudes imposed by natural conditions); the age of science, which had begun with Galileo and Newton and had dominated social thought until the discovery of radium; and the age of the supersensual, which was only just beginning, and in which not only would science dominate the mechanics of existence but in which it would also usurp the realms hitherto commanded by religion, history, and philosophy.[32] Each age had been shorter than its immediate predecessor, and the final era promised to be the shortest of all.

The instinctive era of human development had come to its termination when the force of attraction had drawn together "these trickling rivulets of energy" into a new phase which "tended to concentrate and accelerate . . . motion."[33] The energies of instinct were then transmuted into the energies of religion. The exact time when this transition took place is not made clear, but obviously it must have been somewhere in the mists that separate prehistory from recorded times. It could be Egypt at 4241 B.C., Mesopotamia, or China. The place and exact time were unimportant. What was significant was the

---

[32] Ralph H. Gabriel, *The Course of American Democratic Thought*, 264; Henry S. Commager, *The American Mind*, 287. There is some disagreement among scholars over the precise divisions that Adams wished to make in history, although there is general agreement concerning the broad outlines he intended. Gabriel sees only two major divisions, with the dividing point at 1660. He would further subdivide the scientific age into mechanical, electrical, and ethereal eras. This last era would coincide with Commager's designation of the age of the supersensual. Since Adams, himself, is vague about exact divisions, the four-stage division amplified in the text is a reasonable assumption.

[33] H. Adams, "The Rule of Phase," in *Degradation*, 293.

consolidation of individual energies into a corporate and homogeneous mass. Such concentration was the basis for the new age of religion.

The religious phase of civilization was in the Western world the age of medievalism. It was this period which so attracted Adams and evoked his best single historical work, *Mont-Saint-Michel and Chartres*. It was a time which often seemed at rest and peaceful to the modern man so harried in an earth of unspeakable complexity. And while it did represent a moment when the thought of the world was more unified than it would ever be thereafter, it was still a time when acceleration was manifest. The supernaturalism which permeated the entire epoch was not as pervasive as a first glance might indicate. The thirteenth century was the point of equilibrium—a time when all energy seemed to coalesce in the cross and cathedral; but the balance was a precarious one, and the slightest amount of pressure shook the entire structure. Medieval history is filled with examples of such shock waves: the rise of the papacy, the collapse of the Carolingian empire, the struggle over lay investiture, the onrush of the Turks, and finally the Renaissance. All contributed to the accelerated plunge that history was making toward modern times. The trend away from religion had begun simultaneously with the erection of a God-oriented society. There was a vast difference between St. Augustine and Lord Bacon. By 1660 another transition had been accomplished. Society entered a new phase at an increased speed. The age of science, disencumbered from the strictures of theology and Aristotle, came of age with Kepler, Galileo, and Sir Isaac Newton. Medieval unity had been shattered; a new equilibrium was needed. Science replaced God in the cosmos, and on earth the change was symbolized by substituting mathematics for the cross.

The fact that historical movement was proceeding at an ever

increasing pace was evident, and Adams believed that the solution for predicting the rate of acceleration lay in applying the law of inverse squares. Strangely, it was easier to measure movement for the period since 1660 than to evaluate earlier epochs. It was most applicable for the nineteenth century. Adams reasoned that if the rule proved an accurate measure for this hundred years, then it could be used by the historian as a standard instrument and would oblige him to accept it as a general law for all history. Satisfied that his measuring stick was the correct one, Adams calculated that the age of science could be divided at 1900. The period from 1660 to 1900 he classified as the mechanical phase. The next phase, which he dubbed electrical, was to last for only seventeen years. Then, "it would pass into another or Ethereal Phase and would last . . . about four years."[34] Thus the absolute limit of thought would be reached by 1921 (somewhat later he would revise his estimate to 1927).[35] Exactly what Adams meant by the "electrical phase" and "ethereal phase" was never made completely clear; however, it is a reasonable conclusion that he was referring to new types of energy. Such a conclusion has been reached by many critics who like to see Henry Adams as one who predicted the discovery of atomic energy. It is a deduction which has considerable merit.

The application of the laws of degeneration and phase to history brought Adams to the terminus of his historical work. He was not pleased with what he thought he had discovered. His heritage, his patriotism, and his deep humanity all rebelled at the prospect he had disclosed. His pessimism, which was so much a part of his nature, had found substantial confirmation; but there was no rejoicing by the elder statesman. It was a sad time, with nothing to do but wait for the climax. Henry Adams

[34] *Ibid.*, 302.
[35] H. Adams, *Education*, 341.

knew that he would not be around to witness it, but there was only "another generation to spare before force, space, and time should meet."[36]

There have been many critical attempts at assessing the validity of the laws Henry Adams proposed for history. There have been also a large number of investigations made concerning the motives which compelled him to make the search for laws of history. Critics have found it impossible to separate the motive from the law. Most have tried to interpret the search for historical truth as a manifestation of Adams' own personality. This has been especially true of those who prefer to view him as a literary artist rather than as a historian. But it must be remembered that he was both. These twin facets of his mind refuse to be compartmentalized. Whether Adams made the quest for certainty because of an inner philosophical compulsion or to satisfy the innate curiosity of the historian can never be fully determined. All that can be done is to examine his laws as objectively as possible in light of the reasons he had for engaging in the effort which produced them.

Certainly, no one can read either *The Education of Henry Adams* or *Mont-Saint-Michel and Chartres* without sensing that the search of Henry Adams was intensely personal. These volumes record more than the labors of an industrious historian; they also sketch a philosophic journey. Adams' necessity to extract the meaning from life has a remarkable resemblance to the similar drive in Herman Melville, and one writer claims that the quest of Henry Adams "was as romantic as those of Ahab for Moby Dick or Parsifal for the Holy Grail."[37] There is much

---

[36] *Ibid.*

[37] Robert E. Spiller, "Henry Adams: Man of Letters," *Saturday Review of Literature*, Vol. XXX (February 22, 1947), 11.

truth in this charge, for a presupposition of pessimism is hope. The complete detachment of the scientific observer is neither pessimistic nor optimistic—only impartial. To become pessimistic the investigator must have originally held some hope that his studies would either reinforce his hope or negate his fears. There can be little doubt that Henry Adams must earnestly have desired faith. His study of history was one technique employed to find a basis for faith. He did not succeed. Many others looked at the same history and came away confident of some optimistic absolute such as God or progress. Why did Henry Adams see only decay, degeneration, and death?

The search which Adams made for an active faith was doomed to failure even before he made it. The early denial of his Puritan heritage was the conditioning factor. The disillusionment with the watered-down piety of New England Calvinism left him with an acute distaste for traditional religion. But while he denied the inner truth of the Puritan hypothesis, he was never completely free from its prejudices. It was this which prevented him from embracing the medieval Catholicism to which he was strongly attracted. Moreover, he had substituted science for religion as a faith, and when science failed to provide all the necessary answers, he could not make the required readjustment. He played the human game of constant questioning and searching to the end, but he played it without any real hope of illumination. The closest he ever came to a personal solution to the problem of life "was sincere humility before what he did not know."[38] The two best tools that man had devised—religion and science—had failed to bring order into a chaotic universe. His investigation of both had only confirmed his original fear, that the world and the men within it were the purposeless victims of a capricious fate. He accepted the verdict by formulating a scientific law for history and then

[38] James Stone, "Henry Adams' Philosophy of History," *New England Quarterly*, Vol. XIV (September, 1941), 538-48.

by abandoning science. The rational-romantic split in his personality persevered to the end.

The ultimate impact upon American historiography of his work in forming historical laws will be dealt with in the concluding chapter; however, some remarks should be made here concerning the validity of the laws themselves. At the outset it can be definitely stated that the law of degeneration and the rule of phase were not the definitive answers that their author intended. They were filled with many unexplained gaps, and they demonstrated an incomplete understanding of the scientific ideas they attempted to expound. Also, what has happened since 1900 in the field of atomic physics has greatly altered our concept of the universe; consequently, many of Adams' theories are no longer valid. The development of the laws of relativity have rendered obsolete much of the scientific data which Adams accepted without question. His inability to distinguish between scientific fact and scientific theory, coupled with his desire to apply without much excuse the hypotheses of one area of human knowledge to the totally different dimensions of another, betray the amateur quality of his undertaking. In the field of physics Henry Adams was a novice, and his essay on phase illustrates his lack of professional comprehension.

Yet, despite the objections to any total acceptance of the theorems, their considerable merit and their utility to the historian has been demonstrated. It is true that scientists are no longer positive about the absolute degradation of energy in the universe; however, the application of that principle was extremely accurate in determining certain historical problems. Moreover, it acted as a powerful deterrent to the excesses committed by the zealous proponents of evolutionary history. An entire theory does not have to be accepted in its total implications; some of its more usable parts may be employed with gratifying results. The Newtonian system of celestial mechanics did not explain the fluctuations in the solar orbit of the planet Mercury, but it was precisely accurate in calculating the orbits of other planets. Truth does not have to be a solitary absolute, and the laws of Henry Adams when applied to history may reveal truth in some areas and fail in others.

It may be true, as Van Wyck Brooks maintains, that Adams' concept was "a vast and intricate rationalization . . . an excuse for his own existence."[39] It may even be correct to say with Howard Mumford that Adams was never serious, that he intended only to show historians the dangers of overemphasis on science.[40] These make little difference. Whatever motives there might have been, the laws of Henry Adams represent the most formidable attempt yet made by an American historian to manufacture a scientific law for history. The failure of the laws to be universally true does not cheapen the magnificence of the attempt nor obscure the challenge which Henry Adams hurled at historians. It is a challenge still unanswered.

[39] *New England: Indian Summer*, 481.
[40] "The Tendency of History," *New England Quarterly*, Vol. XXXII (March, 1959), 79–90.

7.

Brooks *Adams: The Law*

THE EQUATION

THE LAW BY WHICH Brooks Adams sought to explain all of the rich and measureless phenomena of history was first concretely stated in *The Law of Civilization and Decay* and then amplified and expanded in *The New Empire* and *The Theory of Social Revolutions*. Its basic ideas and meanings were not altered by these succeeding volumes; they were simply efforts to explain the significance of the law in more and different circumstances. Adams never doubted the validity of his original pronouncement; his later speculations served only to reinforce his original opinions. He was always certain that his formula was the correct one.

In content the law was eclectic, in that it combined some of the conclusions of economic determinism with the more popular components of Darwinist thought. The net result was an equation for history which was as simple in statement as the events it purported to explain were complex. Henry Adams deciphered the law of his brother by reducing it to the following:

All Civilization is Centralization.
All Centralization is Economy.

Therefore all Civilization is the survival of the most economical or cheapest.[1]

Evidently, Brooks had no quarrel with this interpretation, and it stands as a fairly accurate appraisal. The term "centralization" refers to the consolidation of forces or energies, and the term "economy" implies cheapness or reduction in costs. Brooks, himself, put the basic concepts of his projected law on somewhat more elaborate terms; yet, it still may be reduced to an equation of mathematical simplicity. In summarizing his total view of history, Brooks Adams explained:

> Probably the velocity of the social movement of any community is proportionate to its energy and mass, and its centralization is proportionate to its velocity. Therefore, as human movement is accelerated, societies centralize. In the earlier stages of concentration, fear appears to be the channel through which energy finds the readiest outlet; accordingly, in primitive and scattered communities, the imagination is vivid, and the mental types produced are religious, military, artistic. As consolidation advances, fear yields to greed, and the economic organism tends to supersede the emotional and martial.[2]

Simplified in equation form, the law could be stated as V (*velocity*) $= E$ (*energy*) $+ M$ (*mass*) and C (*centralization*) $= V$ (*velocity*). This, then, was the law which civilization had pursued from the very beginning. It was inexorable and immutable, and the final result would be complete and total decay. The direction of civilization was downward, and it was proceeding toward its destiny at an ever increasing rate of speed.

While the above quotation was an effective capsule-summary of Adams' theory, the terms which he employed and the contextual meaning of his hypotheses as they are related to history

---

[1] H. Adams to B. Adams, April 2, 1898, in Ford, *Letters*, II, 163.
[2] *The Law of Civilization and Decay*, 6.

merit some explanation and interpretation. The very ease with which the law may be stated is in itself misleading, as the major premises rest on exceedingly complicated foundations which belie the facility of their enunciation. Each aspect of the theory needs to be analyzed, and, if possible, some determination should be reached concerning the precise nature of the law. If any reasonable evaluation of the law is to be made, it must be done on such a basis. Also, it is a practical necessity for anyone desirous of following the logic of Brooks Adams to understand exactly what is connoted by the special descriptive terms that he uses. Often these words, if not carefully studied, will lead the investigator onto foreign paths. Although never as devious as his brother Henry, Brooks was not as simple and straightforward as he seemed. He was, like most men, a complex personality, and his theory about history reflected his own multiplicity.

The first axiom of the law, that social velocity or movement was proportionate to the energy and mass of a society, had as its base the "accepted scientific principle that the law of force and energy is of universal application in nature." All animal life, Adams maintained, was one of the outlets through which solar energy was dissipated. Since human life was but a form of animal existence, it too was such an outlet. It also followed that these human societies "must differ among themselves in energy, in proportion as nature has endowed them, more or less abundantly, with energetic material."[3] Neither collective nor individual man could escape the consequences of this natural law. Society had only been endowed with a limited quantity of energy; history moved in the cycles as the energy was expended. In such a process the individual counted for nothing. All that he could do was to discover the direction of movement and adjust himself to it. Moreover, since the ratio between velocity and energy-mass was a proportionate one, the

[3] *Ibid.,* 6.

larger the society in terms of both size and energy endowment, the faster would be the social velocity.

As a corollary to this first postulate, Adams also declared that the energy of any society would manifest itself in one of two ways, depending upon which cycle of history was dominant. In the period which was controlled by fear or religion, energetic manifestations could be noted best in artistic and military achievements. In the period where greed was the determinant, expenditures of energy could be seen in the accumulation of wealth. In the first stage art and architecture were the social barometers which reflected "with the subtlest delicacy those changes in the forms of competition which enfeeble or inflame the imagination." In ancient Greece, for example, architecture had told the tale of civilization "more eloquently than any written book."[4] During the second stage money became more important than the fear of the unknown. Consequently, wealth in motion (buying and selling) became the hallmark of an energetic output. Eventually in modern society credit would perform a similar function. Adams also accepted the notion that hoarded capital was, in effect, stored energy and could be "transferred from community to community, either by conquest, or by superiority in economic competition."[5]

The second significant premise inherent in Adams' law was that the centralization of any society was proportionate to its velocity. Since all society is in movement or has velocity, it was obvious, thought Adams, that the movement had direction. That direction was identified as being toward centralization or consolidation. These two words, as Adams used them, were synonymous. They denote a coalescence of social energies which find their expression in those symbols which represent the agencies of power in the society. At the beginnings of organized human culture fear was the controlling factor; it pro-

---

[4] *Ibid.*, 300; B. Adams, *The New Empire*, 31.
[5] *The Theory of Social Revolutions*, 13.

duced superstition, which in turn produced religion. The speed of this process was precisely proportionate to the social velocity, which depended on energy and mass. However, Adams also took it as axiomatic that the rate of acceleration toward consolidation increased rapidly. Thus, modern society was racing toward a point of no return much faster than the fourth century had done. It was the acceleration which was of greatest concern because "as movement accelerates societies consolidate, and as societies consolidate they pass through a profound intellectual change."[6]

The great change which thought underwent during the period of consolidation was a transfer of the major motivating force from fear to greed. As long as fear dominated a society, its energy would be concentrated in the orthodox priesthood which allowed the expenditure of social energy in such things as war, relic-collecting, and cathedral-building. But the advent of greed resulted in the displacement of the aforementioned activities with actions geared only to the acquisition of wealth in either money or goods. War might still be a primary activity, but its goal was no longer the extirpation of religious heresy but the defense or conquest of trade routes. The energy which had been developed during the religious age was now more quickly dissipated by war and economic competition. The economic man replaced the imaginative man, much to the detriment of civilization. But nostalgia was wishful thinking; the law of history was irreversible. Society moved from consolidation to consolidation until all energy should be dissipated. Brooks Adams lamented the helplessness of man but believed that "... history gives me no loophole for escape. ... The course of events from the Crusades, and long before, leads in direct sequence to the present crisis, and I cannot avoid it or alter it."[7]

The third great postulate of Adams' law was that the eco-

[6] *Ibid.*, 243.
[7] B. Adams, "Introduction," to H. Adams, *Degradation*, 92.

nomic will always supersede any other social type. This was the most essential point for statesmen to learn. It was a fundamental truth, and all public figures sooner or later had to acknowledge that "if left undisturbed, the mechanism which operates cheapest will in the end supplant all others."[8] Thus, all civilization became more base as time progressed. The ideals, the values, the personalities of later periods represented more efficiency and less waste but not more beauty or more dedication to the better things of life. Adams believed that the economic phase of civilization was the least admirable and the most vulnerable to fragmentation. Never could one say that he was living in the best of all possible worlds because any particular moment in history was in an aesthetic sense a retrogression from some previous time. Nothing is more antithetical to the ideas of Brooks Adams than the theory of progress. Both Adams and Herbert Spencer were stimulated by the speculations of Charles Darwin; yet where Spencer perceived progress, Adams saw regression. Evolution to Adams was a cheapening process, automatic and natural. Man's responsibility before this inevitable movement was not opposition but acceptance. Nations and men must float with the river which swirled forever downward to the ocean of decay.

How long would this process continue? Adams gave no answer which might be accepted as final. He did not pursue the problem of the conservation of energy into the realm of thermodynamics as his brother Henry had done. But he obviously felt that at some future date the universe would be inert and lifeless, having exhausted its total supply of energy. Limited to human history, the law of civilization and decay was cyclical in nature, with each separate civilization or society running the gamut from concentration to decay. When one society became extinct, another rose to take its place until such time that it too had failed to acquire, by trade or war, new sources of energy.

[8] B. Adams, *The New Empire*, 154–55.

What most historians termed as "rise and fall" Adams believed was more accurately described as "expansion and contraction." Egypt, Babylonia, Greece, Rome, and now the Western Christian civilization had been subjected to the same forces, and their histories revealed similar fates. The modern culture of the West had much to learn concerning its own fate by consulting the decline of Rome, for Brooks Adams fervently believed that Western civilization was reaching the same crucial point in 1895 that Rome had reached with the Empire in 200 A.D. Only by adapting itself to the ceaseless movement of time could it hope to survive.

In writing of the decline and fall of Rome, Brooks Adams said:

> . . . as civilization advances, unless the scientific or inventive qualities which enable men to create wealth, or to suppress waste, gain in at least an equal ratio to the progress of centralization, a centralizing community must perish from inanition if it cannot live by plunder. . . . The Romans paid the cost of centralization by robbing others until conquest ceased; then, not being scientific, they could not turn to industry, and being unable to meet their taxes by agriculture alone, they starved.[9]

Rome had died because she had been both unwilling and unable to adapt to changing circumstances and to develop through science and invention the means of acquiring new wealth. Both the Eastern and Western Empires of Rome were so affected; however, in the West disintegration occurred immediately, and in the East a stationary period supervened until Byzantium eventually toppled to exhaustion and the Turks in 1453.

Twentieth-century Western culture now found itself in the same crucial dilemma. Acceleration had been increasing at a

[9] B. Adams, "A Problem in Civilization," *Atlantic Monthly*, Vol. CVI (July, 1910), 26.

progressive rate since the Reformation, but its velocity had enormously intensified in the year 1760, when the plunder which the English had taken from India began to arrive in London. To Brooks Adams this event was so momentous that it "has divided the nineteenth century from all antecedent time."[10] Since that time gigantic new supplies of energy had been unleashed and the danger to Western man was that the "action of these infinite forces on finite minds" would create an unbearable tension which outmoded laws and institutions would be unable to support. Any quickening in the process of acceleration made the necessity for an equally quick readaptation that much more imperative. Adams was aghast at the possible fate which lay in store for Western society. Rome had fallen at a time of great social change, but the tempo of change in the modern world was infinitely greater. Was it not reasonable, then, to expect a much greater catastrophe? The events of the present century would seem to lend credence to the dire predictions of Brooks Adams which were largely neglected in 1895.

In his later works Adams also developed a number of corollaries to his basic law. At least two of these are important enough to deserve special mention, although in each case the corollary is incidental to and derivative from the law. Perhaps the observation which had the most insight was Adams' declaration that a society's administrative mechanism "must be commensurate to the bulk and the mass to be administered."[11] Civilization might literally dissolve if its organizing and enforcement capacity was unable to keep pace with the increasing momentum of a highly centralized society. To Adams this idea had special application to the modern world of the West. Certainly, to anyone who has been half-strangled in the red tape of modern bureaucracy the necessity for efficient administration has been repeatedly demonstrated.

[10] B. Adams, *The Law of Civilization and Decay*, 255.
[11] B. Adams, *The Theory of Social Revolutions*, 204.

The other perceptive thought was the Adams assertion that monopolies were recurrent social phases which depended for their growth and vitality upon the fluidity which capital or energy was able to exercise within the competitive area. Writing in an age which was greatly concerned with monopolies, which attempted to control corporate growth with antitrust legislation, and which practically deified a "trust-busting" president, it was not surprising that Adams addressed himself to such a topic. What he said was a simple statement of logic: that the potentiality for monopoly increased with the amount of capital being expended. Thus, by implication Adams has pointed to the futility of trying to control monopoly once the monopoly has been created. Control can come only by manipulating the flow of capital and the machinery of credit. That the United States eventually adopted such a view was made quite evident in the monetary legislation of the New Deal.

Brooks Adams consistently made much of the fact that his law for history was scientific in its origin and that he was the detached observer who recorded only what he saw and predicted only what he knew lay in the future. Yet as Shakespeare penetratingly observed, excessive protestations may in actuality reveal an opposite concern. The truth of the matter was that Adams was deeply depressed by the repetitive cycles his law suggested. Even more, he felt that he was a man born out of his time. One who so admired the military conquerors and romantic adventurers of the past could hardly be expected to reconcile himself to the modern heroes of an industrial society whose weapons were the merger and the contract instead of the sword and the lance. A man who so passionately believed in the masculine and the active could never view with impassiveness a sequence of events in which ". . . ebullition yields to lassitude, lassitude passes into torpor, and torpor not infrequently ends in death."[12]

[12] B. Adams, *The New Empire*, 198–99.

In as bitter an indictment as any human ever uttered against the destiny of man and man's civilization, Brooks Adams confided his outrage to his brother Henry:

> Out of it all observe that for the first time in human history there is not one ennobling instinct. There is not a barbarian anywhere sighing a chant of war and faith, there is not a soldier to sacrifice himself for an ideal. How can we hope to see a new world, a new civilization or a new life. To my mind we are at the end; and the one thing I thank God for is that we have no children.[13]

For Brooks Adams, as for T. S. Eliot, the world was to end with a whimper, not a bang.

THE APPLICATION

Adams applied the law of civilization and decay to every conceivable historical situation, and he always felt that it completely met the test. Not only did he find the law suitable for the events of the past, but also he considered it a sure mechanism for analyzing the social problems of the present and for predicting the trends of the future. In his application, however, he formulated two rules which charted the movement of societies from centralization to sterility. The first was that historical movement followed the lines of weakest resistance, and the second was that the path of civilizations had followed the trade routes of the world.

The notion that history sought the lowest level of resistance was indeed compatible with the idea that all civilization tended toward the most economical, although such a doctrine was an obvious simplification of a law of physics, and such transference from one discipline to another can never be made with complete

[13] Quoted in Daniel Aaron, "Brooks Adams: The Unusable Man," *New England Quarterly*, Vol. XXI (March, 1948), 13.

assurance that results will be similar. The doctrine of least resistance to Adams was a great law of nature which men were incapable of violating. Thus, Marcus Aurelius had been impelled to follow the instinct of heredity and had selected his son Commodus to succeed him as emperor in 180 A.D., despite the obvious administrative deficiencies of the latter.[14] Institutions as well as individuals obeyed the law; judicial bodies were perhaps the best examples in that they discriminated "among suitors in proportion to their power of resistance."[15] But all mankind and all history were subject to the same command. For Adams this phenomenon of movement had the greatest significance when applied to the movements of civilizations from one geographic area to another. Civilization, he claimed, followed trade, and trade always proceeded along the lines of least resistance.

A high culture always developed at the center of commercial exchanges because here movement was rapid and men's minds were stimulated. Then, when trade routes shifted "the stimulant is reduced, and proportionate languor supervenes."[16] Communities which have long been abandoned by their trade routes may retain their wealth for long periods of time if they are undisturbed, but they will eventually lose their energy and die. Rome and Byzantium were examples that could be drawn from the ancient world, while the growth of Russia and Japan in the nineteenth century illustrated the validity of the trade-route hypothesis. The rise of the Mediterranean cities, especially Venice, to commercial supremacy in the twelfth century and the subsequent development of the Rhine and Elbe River avenues of trade as thoroughfares to the cities of the Hanse seemed to prove to Adams that his trade-route theory was correct. The best corroborating evidence, however, was to be found in the

---

[14] B. Adams, *The Emancipation of Massachusetts*, 108.
[15] B. Adams, *The Theory of Social Revolutions*, 107.
[16] B. Adams, *The New Empire*, 74.

rise of England to commercial predominance after 1600. Along the way to such a point of eminence Spain, Holland, and France had been defeated in war and by economic competition. And the British Isles had become the seat of international exchanges. Nor was the end of the movement in sight; the United States had by 1900 replaced England. Since the movement of trade had been forever from south to north and from west to east, the world must look to China for the next development, for China would be "the greatest prize of modern times."[17] These, then, were the conditioning factors for detecting historical movement. Within such a framework Brooks Adams rigorously applied the law he had discovered to the different chronological periods of Western history.

In the ancient world the eternal enigma of Rome afforded the best example, although the previous epochs which had involved Egypt and Mesopotamia also seemed to fit the pattern. Adams maintained that the beginnings of Rome's march to greatness could be discovered in the decentralized life of the early Latin farmers. But early in their history another type was developed, the economic man "at once more subtle of intellect and more tenacious of life than the farmers."[18] Had this latter type achieved an early supremacy Rome's downfall might have been delayed, since the economic man was better able to adapt to economic competition. But Rome remained primarily agricultural, and when the Roman farmer was forced to compete with cheaper labor (the slave), he was forced into poverty and the backbone of the Roman system was destroyed. The fall of the Roman republic and the rise of Julius Caesar in the first century before Christ were the outward symbols of the inner calamity. The Empire which followed represented Rome in the age of consolidation—an age in which Rome was forced to live off the conquests she had made. Her native supply of en-

[17] *Ibid.*, 190.
[18] B. Adams, *The Law of Civilization and Decay*, 9.

ergy had been exhausted. After 250 A.D., Rome had lost both political and commercial supremacy.

Roman decay was best exemplified in the extinction of the military type, which was the greatest single essential for the survival of a society. After the first century of the Empire, "Rome not only failed to breed the common soldier, she also failed to produce generals." The abortive attempts of emperors like Marcus Aurelius, Diocletian, and Constantine to revive the waning imperial power were but the last fragmentary bursts of an exhausted energy. By the year 400 A.D. disintegration had almost accomplished its work. The Empire crumbled not because of moral degeneration and corruption but "because the most martial and energetic race the world had ever seen had been so thoroughly exterminated by men of the economic type of mind." Rome fell because she was not able to develop swiftly enough to keep step with her own fast rate of consolidation. Brooks Adams avowed that there had been no barbarian conquest but only "a resolution of an economic consolidation into its elements."[19]

Following the death of the Roman Empire in the fifth century there occurred another period of decentralization, in which once again the priest and the warrior dominated. This was the imaginative era of the Middle Ages, which served as a prelude to the society that is still in existence. From 500 to 1000 A.D. medieval Europe was cut off from the trade routes of the East and was thus able to develop a fairly homogeneous society —one that was slow in its rate of acceleration, as compared to imperial Rome which had preceded it. Ironically, Adams noted that it had been the very religious enthusiasm of the time which had resulted in the pilgrimages. This in turn had restored communication with the East and a consequent acceleration that culminated in the modern centralization. The mammoth pilgrimages which became the Crusades in the twelfth century

[19] *Ibid.*, 39, 44; B. Adams, *The New Empire*, 43.

were the opening wedge in destroying the power of the clergy which had seemed at its epitome in 1100. New economic forces were unleashed, new routes of trade were established, and new ideas culminating in the Renaissance and Reformation destroyed the old order based on fear and replaced it with a new order whose motive was avarice. Just as Rome had seen the warrior supplanted by the usurer, so now the priest had to give up his position to the capitalist. A new consolidation had taken hold, and Western society began the familiar pattern of rapid acceleration.

The most spectacular aspect of this period of increased concentration was the unbelievable growth and development of the small island of England between 1500 and 1800. According to Adams, this phenomenon outshone all others in illustrating what could happen if a nation took advantage of the forces of consolidation. England lay advantageously at the point where the ocean routes of China, India, and America converged. As a manufacturing center, England also sold goods both east and west. No position could have been stronger. Too, the English had made the most of their opportunities. They were among the first peoples, said Adams, to discard completely the fetters of religion. The English Reformation, accurately foreshadowed by John Wycliffe and the Lollard movement, divested the Church of political power and property. Changes in Church doctrine were gradual, only becoming more extreme with each successive spoliation. A new type was created to replace the old clerical hierarchy—a type which with amazing swiftness adapted itself to the new situation. For the Mores, Wolseys, and Cranmers were substituted the Dudleys, Cecils, and the Boleyns. These were the people "who were destined finally not only to dominate England, but to shape the destinies of the world."[20]

[20] B. Adams, *The Law of Civilization and Decay*, 154, 207, 211. The point which Adams makes here is that the Lollards, by denying the miracle of trans-

The effect of the new economic emphasis was to propagate the economic type, to force England into the colonial race, and to increase demands for an ever cheaper religion. The establishment of the American colonies, the Puritan revolution at home, and the rapid pushing of the enclosure movement were all the results of the enormous transformation which had taken place. England was successful in beating off the challenges of Spain and France and by the middle of the eighteenth century seemed practically invincible. Brooks Adams declared that so stable was the English position that decay might have been postponed indefinitely had not the English, themselves, invented the locomotive. This presaged a new and vaster acceleration in the consolidating process, which was to result in the transfer of power from England to America.

At the same time that England was becoming the world's greatest power two other national entities within the Western community fell by the wayside, despite the fact that they too were in favorable geographical areas and could profit from trade-route convergence. Brooks Adams ascribed the fates of Spain and France to their failure to be aware of the nature of the consolidating process. Spain had possessed great martial qualities, but "the Spaniards seem to have been incapable of attaining the same velocity of movement as the races with which they had to compete."[21] The Spanish had not been able to develop the economic type, and in consequence they never centralized. France was hampered more by her archaic administrative structure than an inability to produce the necessary human adaptation. Certainly a nation which could boast of the genius of a Colbert had possessed individuals as capable of meeting the

---

substantiation, had unintentionally shown the way for the monied class to discard the most important hold which religion had on the people. By attacking the miracle Wycliffe was striking at the very heart of religious dominance.

[21] *Ibid.,* 234.

new situation as the English. It was the deficiency of her governmental mechanism which had resulted in chronic insolvency. When this yoke was torn off in 1789, and France under Napoleon made a spectacular bid to catch up with her rivals, it was too late. By 1815 the center of the world's economic exchanges was already in the process of shifting from London to New York.

Adams also believed that his law of civilization and decay was applicable in isolated situations or in specific instances not necessarily connected with the mainstream of civilizations. The law was valid in explaining the movement of Russian history from the river states of Kiev and Novgorod which stood for centralization, through the Slavic and Tartar invasions which meant decentralization, to the new centralization of the fifteenth century during the reign of Ivan III. The rise and fall of the Puritan theocracy in New England could also be interpreted in a similar manner. To Brooks Adams' deterministic mind the fall of the theocracy was inevitable because it had failed to take into consideration problems of economics as well as morals.[22]

The American presidential election of 1828 seemed to provide additional support for a thesis which had as one of its postulates the idea that the cheaper always emerged victorious. Adams might be excused of some prejudice in this matter since his grandfather, John Quincy Adams, had been the losing candidate. Nevertheless, the explanation which Brooks Adams gave for his ancestor's defeat was that "by 1828, a level of degradation had been reached, and it was the level of Jackson."[23] The intelligence and intellectual energy of the democratic community had reached a state of ennui from which not even an Adams could rescue it.

On a micrometric scale the rapid growth of Japan during the

[22] B. Adams, *The Emancipation of Massachusetts*, 385.
[23] B. Adams, "Introduction," to H. Adams, *Degradation*, 84.

latter half of the nineteenth century was an abbreviated but excellent example of the law in operation. Japan's movement had been typical of the age of electricity and steam, when consolidation of energetic resources could take place much quicker. In a single generation the Japanese had reorganized government, education, commerce, industry, and the armed forces. And since "a nation usually concentrates its energy in the highest degree on war, perhaps the institution most emblematic of modern Japan is her army."[24] Moreover, Japan represented the Western influence in the Orient, and Adams predicted that a struggle for survival was impending in the Far East between Japan and Russia, who represented the Eastern motif. Furthermore, such an East-West conflict might prove to be the greatest of catastrophes because "the shock to existing institutions and nationalities would probably approximate in severity any crisis through which civilization has passed."[25]

Finally, in noting the applications which Adams made of the law, it should be mentioned that there were several side effects of its movement which he felt both the historian and the average American citizen should ponder. These derivatives dealt with the problems of the family, the community, and the national government. While not important to the basic theses of the law itself, they are significant in the additional evidence they offer supporting previous contentions that Brooks Adams was sincerely interested in the fate of his fellow man and that his patriotism was of a sincere, simple nature. Like Jonathan Swift, Adams has often been castigated as a misanthrope, when, in reality, it was his deep concern for the race which made him so often speak with bitter invective about the foibles and follies of a frivolous mankind.

Adams warned that one of the first omens of a decaying civi-

---

[24] B. Adams, *The New Empire*, 203.
[25] B. Adams, "War and Economic Competition," *Scribner's Magazine*, Vol. XXXI (March, 1902), 352.

lization was the disintegration of family life. Domestic relations lay at the basis of life's reproductive process, and when these relations were disrupted there was real danger that a perilous social fragmentation could result. Both he and Henry Adams thought they detected such developments in the American family. For the community, large or small, Brooks Adams advised the adoption of a liberal nature. Free inquiry was always more successful in producing a progressive movement than was censorship. Conservatism in excess violated a basic tenet of the historical law—namely, that all history was movement.

The national government, he thought, should be obliged to remember at least three essential requirements for its survival. One was the necessity of a long period of maturation if any kind of stability was to be reached. Quickly formed constitutions, revolutionary empires, and hasty republics were likely to perish as suddenly as they had arisen, for such devices were unable to withstand the strain of faction or the slack of war. "Nothing reaches great age that rushes quickly to maturity."[26] Also any government that desired to promise a future stability must maintain equality before the law. All men must stand equally before a nation's tribunals, and, moreover, those "tribunals must be flexible enough to reach those categories of activity which now lie beyond legal jurisdiction."[27] Finally, with that persistence which dominated his entire character, Brooks Adams asked America that she never forget the importance of metals to the development of society. He repeatedly warned that "competing nations seek, along the paths of least resistance, the means which give them an advantage in the struggle for survival, and among these means the minerals, perhaps, rank first." If America was to be one of the nations that survived, she must ever be aware of the importance of metals. If this

[26] B. Adams, "The Embryo of a Commonwealth," *Atlantic Monthly*, Vol. LIV (November, 1884), 610.
[27] B. Adams, *The Theory of Social Revolutions*, 30, 143.

meant either political or economic imperialism, the risk was worth it. The United States must have the capability of meeting the shocking impacts of the new found energies which seemed to be sweeping the world—powers which Adams saw as overwhelming.[28]

Brooks Adams believed not only that he had discovered an important historical law but also that it was universal in its application. Presented with a seemingly relentless logic, his accomplishment, at first glance, appears without weakness. But on closer examination of this elaborate edifice, certain structural weaknesses become visible which force the evaluator to temper his original approbation. The law of Brooks Adams requires a serious and careful examination.

THE EVALUATION

Four major criticisms can be made of Brooks Adams' historical synthesis. While numerous minor and technical deficiencies may also be discovered, the four points cited below constitute the more significant limitations on his theory. They are the following: the inadequacy of the research for a scheme which seeks to explain all history, the acceptance as axioms of ideas which are not proved axioms, the failure to assess the role of personality in history, and the failure to depict man in his totality. Each of these charges represents an item deserving of analysis and consideration.

The amount of research done by Adams on the rise and decline of civilizations was neither as comprehensive nor as profound as was required for the accurate formulation of historical law. Compared with the depth and labor which A. J. Toynbee exhibited in his twelve-volume *Study of History*, the efforts of Adams seem almost insignificant. Whereas Toynbee examined the origin, structure, and development of every possible civil-

[28] B. Adams, *The New Empire*, 189, 175.

ized society (some twenty-one in all), Brooks Adams confined his investigations almost completely to the culture of the West. Only the Age of Rome and the period of the Reformation received anything that approached intensive treatment. Moreover, there remains, after reading Adams, the distinct impression that his survey has been hurried, that he has not scrutinized carefully the sources, and that his search into the past has been more like that of the tourist who, in his haste to see everything, actually sees nothing. Adams did not painstakingly dissect history; he ransacked it.[29] Certainly any history of civilization which barely mentions such societies as those of ancient Egypt, Sumeria, India, and China cannot pretend to be definitive. Nor can a wide range of historical reading and hazardous generalizations ever be considered as acceptable substitutes for extensive research and cautious but provable synthesis. On this basis alone the professional historian would have to reject the law of civilization and decay as a total explanation for the movement of history. However, perhaps the greatest defect which was contained in Adams' philosophy of history was a nearly obsessive tendency to assume as axiomatic propositions which had not been sufficiently weighed and tested. It is this predilection which constantly plagues the serious student.

Three examples drawn from Adams' theories will suffice to illustrate this trait: (1) Adams claimed as a working hypothesis that social energy or thought proceeded from solar energy. It was on this single idea that he was able to justify the search for a law on the grounds that all physical phenomena were explainable by physical laws. As John L. Stewart pointed out, this hypothesis was never proved,[30] nor has it been verified to

---

[29] Stuart P. Sherman, "Evolution in the Adams Family," *Nation*, Vol. CX (April 10, 1920), 476.

[30] John L. Stewart, Review of *The Law of Civilization and Decay* by Brooks Adams, *Annals, American Academy of Political and Social Sciences*, Vol. VIII (July, 1896), 162–67.

the present time. Indeed, until science can develop an instrument which will calculate and measure the relationship between solar and social energy, there can be no scientific justification for believing that such a relationship exists. History still is more for the man of letters than for the white-coated researcher in the laboratory. (2) Adams also asserted with customary vigor that all civilization was an expression of the most economical. In other words, the more concentrated the civilization, the less articulate the culture. Such reasoning carried to its logical ends approaches absurdity. This would imply, for instance, that the best which the artistic mind had to offer could only be encountered at the beginning of a civilized epoch. One must be able to see a steady retrogression from that point. This view ignores the thorny problem of renaissances with which Toynbee has wrestled so violently. What Adams has done is to trust completely his personal aesthetic tastes as infallible guides to what is and is not good artistic expression. Because Brooks Adams considered the romanticism of the Gothic cathedral superior to the functional designs of Frank Lloyd Wright, such is not necessarily the fact. Applied unilaterally, it would be necessary to claim that any poet of the tenth century was superior to any poet in the sixteenth. True, Adams made no such statement; but carried to conclusion, his basic premise concerning the deterioration of civilization would lead to that kind of nonsense. (3) Another of Adams' dogmatisms was the claim that fear, as expressed first in superstition and then in religion, was the impulse which led to cultural achievement and that greed, as expressed in commerce, stifled the creative impulse. For proof he cited the medieval period of Western culture. However, there are countless historians, like H. E. Barnes, who would argue just oppositely and cite Periclean Athens as an example.[31] When discussing the rise of the great city-states

[31] Harry E. Barnes, "Brooks Adams on World Utopias," *Current History*, Vol. VI (January, 1944), 5.

in Italy between the twelfth and fifteenth centuries, Adams ascribed their growth to the new commercial instinct which had stimulated greed. But he conveniently forgot to mention that accompanying this revival of trade were the splendorous accomplishments of the Italian Renaissance. The point to be made is not that Adams was totally in error, but rather that neither was he totally correct. He never perceived the obvious: that life, the universe, and history were infinitely complex and not subject to oversimplification.

Perhaps Brooks Adams might be excused from not stressing the role of personality in history, since his entire theoretical structure was of necessity mechanistic in its concepts. Yet, any historian who explains history without the slightest reference to the role of the individual neglects a primary purpose of historical study. Adams studied the Protestant Reformation of the sixteenth century with but the most casual of references to Luther and Calvin. There was never any admission that personality did, in fact, alter the nature and direction of historical events. Even for the moment granting the truth of his assertion that all humanity was subject to the dictates of natural law, this does not obviate the demonstrable fact that individuals can and do shape the particular character which composes the uniqueness of every happening. Adams, himself, acknowledged the possibility of this when he described the achievement of Alexander the Great.[32] No historian can ever divest his subject matter of the human personality, for, in essence, it is the vital material which produced the history he is studying.

Finally, the fourth major defect lay in Adams' concise but narrow viewpoint of personality. He never saw the whole human being. His conclusion that all of man's drives are motivated by either fear or greed was obviously one-sided and betrayed his Calvinistic orientation. He made no provision for any other motives—ones for which men fight and die. Religion,

[32] B. Adams, *The New Empire*, 36.

love, power, glory, and hate were thrust aside as meaningless.[33] A psychological dichotomy was performed without the benefits of either psychological training or modern statistical techniques. The unqualified statement that humanity has been directed by only two forces could never become more than an observation which was belied by facts that its author chose to ignore.

Nevertheless, despite these serious objections, the law which Brooks Adams expounded contained some positive benefits for the student of history. Certainly no writer has ever so clearly exposited the dramatic role which economic forces play in the shaping of history. It may be true, as Edwin Seligman suggested, that their impact was overemphasized,[34] but there was much truth to be found in Adams' theories concerning the importance of trade routes and minerals in determining the growth of civilizations. His appraisals of the fundamental weaknesses of the American system of industrial capitalism were well taken, as was his critique of the modern judiciary as inadequate for the modern world.

Another meritorious effect was Adams' insistence on seeing history in totality. He wrote in an age which had conveniently fragmented history—usually into national epochs, with the resultant falsification of perspective. Adams insisted that history embraced all societies everywhere. The fact that he, himself, did not always abide by this standard does not lessen the validity of his approach. If the publication of *The Law of Civilization and Decay* had done nothing more than to stimulate controversy about the meaning of *all* history, it would have been worth the effort.

[33] Anonymous, review of *The New Empire* by Brooks Adams, *Outlook*, LXXIII (January 24, 1903), 218–19; Don M. Wolfe, *The Image of Man in America*, 247–48.

[34] Edwin R. A. Seligman, *The Economic Interpretation of History*, 109–10. Henry Adams also thought the economic determinant to be exaggerated and to contain too many unknown factors. See H. Adams to B. Adams, September 7, 1900, in Cater, *Friends*, 499.

In addition, Brooks Adams was responsible for recalling to historians that their profession imposed obligations which too few had met in the nineteenth century. He had reiterated what the great historians of the past had accepted as a normal function: the positive necessity of explaining the past in terms of an honest but meaningful synthesis. It was not enough for the historian to say what had happened; it was also incumbent upon him to say why it had happened and what significance it had for his own generation. Without such goals history was nothing but antiquarianism, and the historian, little more than an amusing tinkerer. Adams had written books filled with material that was suggestive of contemporary problems, and his theory was something that had to be reckoned with by all interested in the nature of history. Judged from this viewpoint, Brooks Adams' historical law was not a failure.

8.

The Laws Compared

THE LAW OF DEGRADATION formulated by Henry Adams and the law of civilization and decay constructed by Brooks Adams were remarkably similar insofar as they both perceived a general degenerative trend to history. Moreover, each had as its starting point a particular concept of energy. For Henry, it was Kelvin's second law of thermodynamics which posited the gradual dissipation of energy; for Brooks, it was the assumption that the earth had been endowed with a specific amount of solar energy which was in the process of being expended by human society. The Adamses likewise deduced that social energy as illustrated by historical movement was one form of the great universal energy and could consequently be calculated according to scientific laws. Both looked to history for confirmation, and each believed that reasonably accurate predictions concerning the course of future history could be made. However, from this point there was considerable divergence of views—differences which were imbedded in the very nature of the laws that had been formed.

Henry's law of degradation never permitted the examination of history as an entity, separate and distinct from its relationship to the energetic laws which governed the universe. Degradation depersonalized history and refused to countenance any isolation of terrestrial matter. The universe, insisted Henry Adams, was an organic whole, of which the history of mankind was but the minutest fragment. However, since it was a part of the whole, it could be expected to conform to the laws which governed the whole. Hence, the only discipline competent to gauge the movement of history was physics. Brooks' law of civilization and decay did not make such a gigantic presumption. While admitting the fact of energy, Brooks Adams preferred to believe that the expenditure of energy in this part of the universe might be more correctly determined by the science of biology. Where Henry had appealed to Kelvin, Brooks sought support from Darwin. The result was that the two laws differed sharply in their angles of vision. Both are looking at the same stream of historical events; yet they see things differently because of the particular viewing device used.

Each law is also especially concerned with the rate of movement at which civilization is propelled through solar time. By applying Brooks' equation, one detects an alternating series of accelerations and decelerations which move in endless cycles. Henry argues that the movement of civilization has been one of ever increasing velocity. He does not use the cyclical idea, nor does he see any merit to his brother's concept of periodic alterations in the relative speed of social movement. Again, the opposing frames which each is employing must be remembered. This helps to explain the variations in theory. To Henry the periods of seeming lassitude followed by recurrent outpourings of energy must be viewed from the more cosmic scale. Energy was never being conserved. All human activity was part of the much larger process always active throughout the universe.

Both theories employed similar terminology. The terms "mass," "velocity," "acceleration," and "concentration" are frequently used to indicate specific meanings. They should not be interchanged without much caution, for what Brooks may mean by "concentration" might well imply something totally different to Henry. Similarly, the Adamses often use identical terms to describe unlike processes or events. Thus, to Henry Adams the "velocity" of history is the speed at which thought or mental activity moves. But to Brooks the "velocity" of history refers to the speed at which a civilization concentrates its energies. At best, then, any comparison of the subject matter of the two laws is a hazardous undertaking. Just as one would be hard-pressed to make a meaningful comparison between any two unlike objects, so it is difficult to compare the theories of Henry and Brooks Adams.

In the application of their laws to the actual historical process each of the Adamses found it convenient to divide all human history into distinct stages or phases. The isolation of history into certain set epochs was something that both writers felt to be dictated by the operation of their respective theorems. Henry Adams divided history into four phases which he called the ages of instinct, religion, science, and the supersensual. Each era had been shorter than the preceding age because of the acceleration and expansion of energies. The final stage was only just beginning and would be the shortest of all. Henry had arrived at this division by applying Willard Gibbs' rule of phase to historical phenomena. He thus hoped to arrive at a reasonably exact estimate of the speed with which the world was moving toward degradation.

Brooks Adams also divided history into separate ages, but whereas Henry discovered four such time periods, Brooks found only two. These were the age of imagination, in which society was dominated by fear of the unknown, and the age of consolidation, in which the motivating force of society was the desire to acquire wealth. However, Brooks saw these two eras as repetitive, recurring in cycles throughout history. Henry had perceived no such cyclical development. His four-stage process was one which embraced the whole of history. But Brooks applied his two-stage movement to every civilization which the world had seen. One important observation which both made was that in the present stage of history, energy was being both consolidated and expended at an enormously faster rate than at any previous time.

In analyzing the factors involved in social movement Henry Adams contended that the most significant was the increase in energy expenditure which had resulted from an acceleration of scientific endeavor. The Middle Ages had been destroyed by the discoveries of the new science, and since that time the rate of social movement had increased in direct ratio to the expansion of science. Moreover, the end result of all movement was inevitable degradation, and the release of new energies by science would only hasten the day when no further expansion would be possible. Modern man had reached a point where he could no longer cope with the forces he had unleashed. They were as mysterious and omnipotent to him as the cross and the cathedral had once seemed in the days of chivalry.

Looking at the same social movement, Brooks Adams decided that the most influential factor had been the trade route. The desire of nations to control the avenues of trade had been the hidden reason in history for the increased rapidity of social movement. Closely connected to the trade route was the importance of metals, which followed the trade route and tended to be stored in those commercial exchanges which invariably dominated the termini of such routes. This fact helped to explain the seemingly ceaseless movement of the centers of exchange from east to west and from south to north. For Brooks the forces revealed by his law of civilization and decay were never as impenetrable as those Henry thought he had glimpsed through his law of degradation. While each brother contended that the forces operative in history could be measured and calculated, Henry Adams was never positive that the precise nature of those forces could be known. Brooks, on the other hand, believed that he not only knew the power and direction of forces but also the character of the forces themselves.

Probably the most noteworthy comparison that can be drawn between the applications of the two laws was that Brooks maintained that his theory had lessons important to contemporary America. Henry did little more than to suggest that modern man was tobogganing to his own destruction. Brooks felt that his destruction might be averted if society would only accommodate itself to the law inherent in civilization. Consequently, he had a plethora of suggestions. The national government must adjust its administrative mechanism so that it was capable of dealing with an expanded economy. The nation's judicial system must sufficiently alter its course to avoid the disruptive character of a social revolution. And, most important, the nation must anticipate the flow of civilization from one trade route to another so that it might maintain its superiority by acquiring the future centers of trade. To Brooks Adams this meant that the United States must become an active participant in the scramble for commercial outposts in Asia and particularly in China. This is why he so completely approved of the Spanish-American War and the resultant acquisition of territory in the Far East. The Philippines became a steppingstone to the eventual control of China. The "open-door" policy announced by John Hay in 1899 was also gratifying to Brooks because it seemed to offer an indication that the United States had every intention of preserving her commercial interests in China.

Henry Adams agreed to some extent with his brother's concern, but he could never become quite as exercised. This was because Henry had resigned himself, at least intellectually if not emotionally, to the fact of eventual degradation. Brooks' proposals would only delay the process; they would not avoid it. Although in logic the law of Brooks Adams admitted the final exhaustion of energy, its formulator did not foresee this in the immediate future. What he saw was the decay of a civilization of which the United States had become the leader. This was what he wished to avert. This was the basic reason for the difference in their attitudes. Henry contended that man and life were near the day of judgment; Brooks believed that the final reckoning was still far in the future.

It would be almost impossible to evaluate on a comparative basis the relative strengths and weaknesses of each of the laws because they were essentially dealing within different frames of reference. However, certain observations can be made that may help to clarify the relationship of the laws to each other. Both laws, if judged in the absolute sense, were failures. That is to say, neither has been proved to be what it pretended—namely, an explanation for all history. History has been shown to be of such complexity that it does not permit of mathematical explanation. In addition, both Adamses made much the same fundamental error in their calculations. They attempted to transfer the hypotheses and deductions from one field of knowledge to another without making special allowances for basically dissimilar situations. Henry Adams attempted to apply laws of thermodynamics and physics to history, and Brooks attempted the same thing with the dicta of biology. This is not to say that such transference is impossible, only that the necessary knowledge for it was not available to permit a successful undertaking in 1900. Nor is such data present in 1960.

Each of the laws has provided historians with unique insights, even though the laws of degradation and of civilization and decay did not prove to be total syntheses. The emphasis which Brooks Adams placed on the significance of the trade route and of precious metals certainly sheds a good deal of light on imperialist motivations. His discussion of the causes of the Reformation, although often superficial and misleading, has illustrated economic forces which deserved recognition. The rhythmic cycles which Brooks outlined have some validity; the work of A. J. Toynbee would seem to confirm this. There is an over-emphasis on Darwinism, and, admittedly, a strict application of evolution to history leaves many things unanswered. But it is also true that the notions of competition and survival of the fittest often explain certain situations. The historian had more insight into his materials after Brooks Adams than before.

Henry Adams worked on a larger scale than did his brother; hence, both his achievement and his failure are of greater proportion. Perhaps the most lasting benefit to the historical profession was Henry's reminder that history is more than a science. For by depersonalizing history and giving it a scientific law, Henry Adams stressed in bold outline the great tragedy of the human race—its subjective nature caught in an objective universe. The great lesson for historians to learn from the law of Henry Adams is one that he himself never completely understood. The true historian must not only have a passionate love for truth but also a profound sympathy and understanding for the human beings who make up his history.

9.

The Adamses
and the American Dream

THE SEARCH AND THE DREAM

THE SEARCH WHICH Henry and Brooks Adams made for the laws of history was a part of a continuing tradition in all forms of literature to discover the fulfillment of the American dream. Furthermore, the failure of the Adamses to find any justification in the pages of history for the possible realization of the dream was part of a general disillusionment with America and her dream which became most manifest after World War I. It was not simple coincidence that made *The Education of Henry Adams* as a handbook for the skeptical much more popular in the twenties than it had been in the previous decade. Both of these hypotheses merit further analysis, but it is first necessary to attempt a definition and identification of this recurring theme, usually termed "the American dream."

There can be no precise definition because the American dream has meant different things to different people. Also, the impulses which have given rise to the term have often been indirect and unconscious.[1] Nevertheless, the dream has been one of the chief motivating forces of American civilization. By distilling the major ideas concerning the dream

[1] Frederic I. Carpenter, *American Literature and the Dream*, 3.

which both writers of belles-lettres and historians have propounded, the central motif appears to be the belief in the possibility of a more perfect democracy. James Truslow Adams defined it as "that dream of a better, richer, and happier life for all our citizens of every rank which is the greatest contribution we have as yet made to the thought and welfare of the world."[2] The words *progress, freedom,* and *democracy* are crucial to its meaning; and the dream always carries with it the connotations of hope and faith. There should be hope in the potentiality of America and a faith in the nation's ability to realize that potentiality.

The images and visions which the dream has produced have been celebrated throughout American history in verse, novel, history, and essay. They have found expression in the speeches of politicians and in the homilies of the clergy. They have to a great extent determined the directions of American culture. Art and literature in America have largely been either the arguments for the promise of American life or expressions in antagonism to such Utopian purposefulness. The democratic faith together with its defenders and attackers has occupied a considerable portion of American thought, and most historians of the development of native ideas have had this faith as their point of departure. No careful examination of American culture or history can safely ignore this great theme without seriously limiting its value; for the American artist, whether he be poet or historian, has reflected the image of the promised land.

American literature really began with the Puritan attempt to create the "City of God" in New England. Despite the fatalistic elements of seventeenth-century Calvinism, there was a dedicated purpose about the men who founded Massachusetts. The fierce zeal of Puritanism, combined with the comparative freedom of a seemingly limitless environment, produced a cul-

2 *The Epic of America,* vii.

ture which was surprisingly optimistic. Even the great divine Jonathan Edwards could not overcome the joy that he discovered in nature. And he was imbued with reverence for what seemed a heaven-sent opportunity to put into operation God's plan for man. Later the more sober Calvinistic tenets of natural depravity and predestination would be modified and mellowed in the face of an environment which seemed to question their reality. By 1820 the devotees of transcendentalism had divested the Puritan heritage of its harsher tenets and had retained only the code of morality which emphasized those virtues deemed essential for progress in the best of all possible worlds. Ralph Waldo Emerson, Henry David Thoreau, and Louisa May Alcott were personifications of the belief that America was a beacon light to an unenlightened world. James Fenimore Cooper and Washington Irving told of the promise that lay in the wilderness, and shortly thereafter, Walt Whitman sang mystically of the democratic faith in the cities. Certainly there were dissenters to this spontaneous optimism; Nathaniel Hawthorne and Herman Melville disclosed the darker sides of human nature, and both questioned the possibility of realizing the American dream in an amoral universe. Yet even in their dissent such men acknowledged the existence of the dream and its pervasive influence upon the American mind.

The more serious objections to American optimism occurred as a result of the rise of industrialism in the post–Civil War United States. The disillusionment of William Dean Howells was the turning point. Spurred by this example, literary naturalists led by Theodore Dreiser began to disclose the shabbiness and poverty of American existence. What justification was there for a faith whose only fruit had been the obvious brutalization of society? Were the sweatshop, the slum, and Wall Street confirmation of the great promise Emerson had imagined in *The American Scholar?* Was it not better to admit that the bright hopes for a more perfect tomorrow had been nothing more than hopes? Yet, despite the mass of evidence which the pessimists compiled, the dream did not fade. A new philosophy was developed which took notice of the deficiencies of American life but argued that something could be done about them. Pragmatism was, in this sense, the heir of the transcendentalist tradition; they were part of the same tradition. The dream survived.

The very movement of American political history likewise proves the existence of the dream. From Jefferson's words in the Declaration of Independence, through Lincoln's second inaugural address, to Franklin D. Roosevelt's famous denunciation of fear, political figures have clung to the notion that in America "lay the last best hope of man." Every phase of our history has been interpreted in light of how well the dream was being realized. Americans have always felt an inner compulsion to see themselves as agents of destiny—a new chosen people who had been charged by their Creator to guide the rest of the world out of the wilderness and into a new promised land. In myriad ways the basic belief in the innate goodness of this fertile country has been exhibited. The westward movement, the fight against slavery, the expansion of the United States, the reform tradition, the progressive movement, the involvements in foreign wars—all have been interpreted as methods by which the nation has reached for the fulfillment of its dream. Our national heroes are those who have best articulated the hope for an ever better world. Jefferson said that one of man's inalienable rights was the pursuit of happiness. Lincoln prayed at Gettysburg that government of, by, and for the people would not perish. Franklin D. Roosevelt told his generation that it had a rendezvous with destiny. The dream persisted; it has been a part of the very bone and sinew of America. It was a part of the Adams family and tradition; it was the drive behind the search for historical certainty conducted by Henry Adams and Brooks Adams. What each sought, in his own way, was historical proof that the American dream could come true. Both failed to find that surety. As a result the course of American historiography was significantly altered.

American historians had also written largely from the optimistic point of veiw before 1890. Composing from either a romantic or patriotic preconception, historians had invariably emphasized the beauty of the democratic society and had pictured the growth of the United States as a process aiming ultimately at the complete realization of democratic hopes. The main theme of George Bancroft was that the spirit of the colonies had demanded freedom. Kraus states that "to Bancroft, the United States was the leader among all nations; no spokesman of the young Republic ever wrote with greater assurance."[3] John Motley injected basic American themes into his history of the Dutch Republic, while the romantic movement reached its climax in the vivid writings of Francis Parkman, who captured for his readers the great abundance and promise at which the vast wilderness of North America had hinted. Both Henry and Brooks Adams reacted against this tradition by subjecting the values and ideals of American society to the closest scrutiny. Indeed, they both discovered what they thought were historical laws, but neither of their laws supported the hopes of the American dream. One saw degradation and the other, decay. And when the search had been completed each was bitterly disappointed, because in their souls the Adams brothers had fervently hoped that the American dream was capable of fulfillment.

THE DREAM INTERPRETED

In their writings and correspondence the Adamses revealed their deep concern with the past, present, and the future of their native land. In fact, it would have been inconceivable

[3] Michael F. Kraus, *The Writing of American History*, 118.

that any member of the Adams family should have felt differently. Both Henry and Brooks were ever conscious of the heritage which was theirs, and the fact that neither had occupied a responsible position in the government was a source of constant regret and some bitterness. It was not, however, the wellspring from which their pessimistic philosophies flowed.[4] Their thoughts and feelings about America were conditioned by what they had studied in her history and by what they had observed in her contemporary society.

Perhaps the most penetrating comment which the Adamses made concerning the American scene was that America was lost. Development had been so rapid that the nation had lost its sense of direction. In a most lyrical passage Henry Adams stated the idea this way:

> Society in America was always trying, almost as blindly as an earthworm, to realize and understand itself; to catch up with its own head, and to twist about in search of its tail. Society offered the profile of a long, straggling caravan, stretching loosely towards the prairies, its few score of leaders far in advance and its millions of immigrants, negroes, and Indians far in the rear, somewhere in archaic time.[5]

Brooks Adams too felt that the United States was fast approaching the point of no return. The headlong consolidation of en-

[4] One of the most widely held conclusions concerning the pessimism of Henry Adams is that since the political world had failed to make use of his talents, Henry was in a perpetual pout. Furthermore, it has been concluded that Henry rationalized his failure by deciding that a society which had rejected him must be of little value. While there is some truth to this charge, on the whole it is far too facile and superficial an explanation. G. H. Roelfos effectively refutes this view by asserting that Henry was deliberately pessimistic in order to awaken America to what was happening to her. Adams, says Roelfos, despaired not because of the powerful forces unleashed in the modern world but because of the inertia of the American mind before such forces. See Roelfos, "Henry Adams: Pessimism and the Intelligent Use of Doom," *Journal of English Literary History*, Vol. XVII (September, 1950), 214–39.

[5] *Education*, 237.

ergies had propelled the nation to an ultimate point of concentration. For the present the country seemed to occupy a position of extraordinary strength. She had been "favored alike by geographical position, by deposits of minerals, by climate, and by the character of her population."[6] But unless there was a reawakening and a rededication, America would lose the lead in the contest for universal supremacy.

Although both Henry and Brooks disliked what they saw in America after 1865, the former was much more deeply affected. Henry could never accept, as Brooks did, conditions in the United States as only simple manifestations of the operation of an inexorable law. Despite the mechanistic character of his later historical commentaries, Henry Adams never became the complete determinist. Brooks was able to accept the implications to which his studies led him, but Henry could never forget what great achievements his country had once promised. What disillusioned him as much as anything else was the deterioration of the promise of American life.[7] A nation which at the beginning appeared to be marching vigorously toward a rewarding destiny now was "wandering in a wilderness much more sandy than the Hebrews had ever trodden about Sinai." It had sold its birthright for railroad land grants and multiple corporations. Intellectually, the country was barren. "It shunned, distrusted, disliked, the dangerous attraction of ideals, and stood alone in history for its ignorance of the past."[8]

Certainly, there was not much in American life in those tumultuous postwar years to warrant any optimism. People with only a modicum of sensitivity and perception must have been appalled at the face of the new nation. All around them they saw the vices attendant to party loyalty and the spoils system; they saw elevated to high positions the ignorant and the im-

[6] B. Adams, *The New Empire*, xxxiii.
[7] Hamilton Basso, "A Mind in the Making," *New Yorker*, Vol. XXIII (March 29, 1947), 105.
[8] H. Adams, *Education*, 328.

moral; they saw the depressing tendency to reduce all society to one low level; and they saw the snobbery of the *nouveau riche* and the greedy machinations of corrupt politicians. Americans had embarked on the pursuit of profit to the exclusion of everything else, and Henry Adams declared that he, for one, would ". . . be glad to see the whole thing utterly destroyed and wiped away."[9]

Even Brooks was forced to admit that something had gone wrong. In writing of those sixty years that had witnessed the tremendous events of the Seven Years' War, the American Revolution, the French Revolution, and the Napoleonic Wars, Brooks claimed that none had been as momentous as "the rise of the United States as a nation."[10] The full realization of the democratic ideal had seemed definitely in prospect. Everything had been favorable. Americans had been presented with unlimited natural resources and freedom from external pressure. "The only serious problem for them to solve, therefore, was how to develop this gift on a collective and not on a competitive or selfish basis."[11] Yet, the country had refused the chance. Before the Civil War democracy had been forced to compromise by uniting itself with a slaveholding oligarchy, and in postwar times it had fallen victim to the unchecked forces of competition. The great dream of a democratic Utopia was gone. Brooks was willing to go on from there—to make the best of the situation. Henry was too much a part of the eighteenth century. He had no desire to proceed any farther.

One facet of the national character which both brothers deplored was the provincialism which permeated most areas of American life. The tendency of Americans to regard suspiciously anything foreign had kept the country from partaking

[9] H. Adams to Elizabeth Cameron, September 15, 1893, in Ford, *Letters,* II, 33.
[10] B. Adams, "Convention of 1800 with France," *Proceedings, Massachusetts Historical Society,* Vol. XLIV (February, 1911), 378.
[11] B. Adams, "Introduction," to H. Adams, *Degradation,* 80–81.

in the main currents of Western civilization as much as would have been desirable. The natural isolation provided by environment had been, therefore, both a blessing and a curse. It had provided a good incubator for the democratic experiment, but it had also blighted artistic and literary development by depriving the creative arts of many of the new ideas which arose in Europe. Brooks believed that "we have never overcome that trait of provincialism. For an American author to receive credit in his own country, he must first win reputation abroad."[12] And Henry repeatedly departed from the nation's capital for trips to Europe, convinced, as S. P. Delany suggests, of "the futility of Boston, the vulgarity of Washington, the bleakness and aridity of Puritanism, the coldness and desolation of Protestantism, the necessary limitations of democracy, the illusion of progress and the flimsiness of our scholarship."[13]

Yet, no matter how much they decried the American lack of vision and sophistication, the Adamses were curiously ambivalent on the subject. Brooks, who had denounced provincial traits so strongly, often exhibited a basic conservatism which bordered on the superpatriotic. He contended that only a thoroughgoing Yankee could ever write a truly American novel, and he cited Shakespeare and Sir Walter Scott as examples of writers who were great because they had been thoroughly English and had cared little for foreigners.[14] Furthermore, Brooks urged upon his compatriots a program of self-sacrifice "if we would have our civilization, our country, our families, our art, and our literature survive."[15] Neither could Henry ever escape the deep patriotism he held for America. When he was

[12] *Ibid.*, 46.

[13] "Man of Mystery," *North American Review*, Vol. CCXVI (November, 1922), 704.

[14] B. Adams, Review of *The Undiscovered Country* by William Dean Howells, *International Review*, Vol. IX (August, 1880), 149–54.

[15] B. Adams, "The American Democratic Ideal," *Yale Review*, Vol. V (January, 1916), 232.

absorbed in writing or studying American history, his feelings often approached reverence. The historian, he maintained, should often shut his eyes and:

> . . . become conscious of a silent pulsation that commands his respect. . . . As one stands in the presence of this primitive energy, the continent itself seems to be the result of agencies not more unlimited in their power, not more sure in their processes, not more complete in their result, than those which have controlled our political system.[16]

One need only read any of his writings on American history to realize that Henry Adams intensely loved his country, even though the intensity was covered with a feigned indifference.

The failure of the United States to solve with good sense many of the enormous problems which confronted her was another factor cited by the Adamses as evidence of the nation's refusal to come to grips with its own fate. Americans had lost the inner dynamism and sense of ultimate values which had characterized her earlier history. Since most of the material needs of life were being supplied in abundance, the country saw little necessity in beginning an assault on problems that were nonmaterial in nature. Prosperity had been mistaken for paradise; standards of living had become confused with standards of conduct. The people had forgotten, said Brooks Adams, that the closest synonym for democracy was unselfishness. Those problems which seemed the most disturbing were the situation of the South, the growing inequality in the class structure, the tendency toward monopoly and concentration of capital, and the drift toward a collective state.

To both Henry and Brooks Adams the South represented that section of the country which was the most retarded and had

[16] H. Adams and Henry Cabot Lodge, Review of *A History of the United States* by Hermann Von Holst, *North American Review*, Vol. CXXIII (October, 1876), 361.

played the major role in wrecking the American dream. Although they shared this antipathy, the two brothers differed somewhat in their reasoning. Brooks attacked the South for what he considered its economic folly. Its financial stupidity, he maintained, had begun when "the aristocracy of the South deliberately chose a civil war rather than admit the principle that at some future day they might have to accept compensation for their slaves."[17] They had chosen to see their section wasted and devastated rather than adapt themselves to the new conditions which had been imposed by industrialism. The entire aristocratic leadership of the South had perished in the ensuing holocaust, at a time when it still had much to contribute to the nation. America had been the loser, however, for the South had become only an embarrassing appendage. Henry's complaint was that the South always acted from irrationality and ignorance. His observation of Robert E. Lee, Jr., at Harvard might well have been applied to the South as a whole:

> Strictly, the Southerner had no mind; he had temperament. He was not a scholar; he had no intellectual training; he could not analyze an idea, and he could not even conceive of admitting two; but in life one could get along very well without ideas if one had only the social instinct.[18]

No one, thought Henry, could ever rightly question Southern courage, but the Southern people themselves consistently had demonstrated that they thought courage was limited to Dixie. Henry lamented that they "owed their ruin chiefly to such ignorance of the world."[19] Whatever the motives for Southern intransigence, the Adamses felt the South to be a perpetual blight on the advancement of America. Moreover, nothing was being done about it.

[17] B. Adams, *The Theory of Social Revolutions*, 33.
[18] H. Adams, *Education*, 57–58.
[19] *Ibid.*, 188.

As has been previously noted, it was Brooks Adams who was the more concerned with the growing class inequality which, he felt, revealed itself most dramatically in the weaknesses of the judiciary. America was blind, according to Brooks, to the dangers resulting from an age of unbridled capitalism. Capital had begun using the sovereign power to pursue its private interests, and this usage was most manifest in the actions of judges. Brooks averred that in the course of time the federal judiciary had become increasingly involved in politics and the result had been "not to elevate politics, but to lower the courts toward the political level."[20] He feared the courts had lost awareness that they had been created as servants of the people and not as the willing tools of those powerful few who desired to be the people's masters. What was additionally alarming was that this insidious obeisance to one favored class had penetrated the very citadel of the American constitutional system—the Supreme Court.

Brooks Adams contended that the Supreme Court was the cornerstone on which the entire national edifice had been constructed. "Without an independent judiciary, constitutional limitations are a mockery, for there can be no other curb on the majority."[21] The high tribunal was well on its way to becoming an upper chamber whose duties were to preserve and maintain the vested interests of the wealthy. Assailing the complacency of the legal profession when faced with this development, Brooks complained that American lawyers now believed "that a sheet of paper soiled with printer's ink and interpreted by half-a-dozen elderly gentlemen snugly dozing in armchairs, has some inherent and marvellous virtue by which it can arrest the march of omnipotent nature."[22] Brooks, of course, was only echoing the plea for sociological jurisprudence which had al-

[20] *The Theory of Social Revolutions*, 45–46.
[21] B. Adams, "The Supreme Court and the Currency Question," *International Review*, Vol. VI (June, 1879), 643.
[22] *The Theory of Social Revolutions*, 214–15.

ready been so eloquently stated by Oliver Wendell Holmes—
an ideal which would subsequently be realized. But at the turn
of the century matters looked bleak, and Brooks Adams warned
that either there would be absolute equality before the law, or
the masses would seek social justice beyond the law.

Henry Adams was also concerned with the problems presented by the concentration of capital and the growth of monopoly; however, his concern did not center itself on the judiciary. What disturbed the elder brother was the rather vague
feeling that a complete capitulation to capitalism with its attendant industrial machinery would be the finishing stroke for
the agrarian America which had seemed to offer so much.
Henry was dissatisfied with entrepreneurs and masters of capital not because they lacked morality but because they represented a cheapening of the American image which had remained
intact since the days of the early republic. This attitude, more
than any other he possessed, revealed how fondly Henry Adams
had regarded the great American dream.

For Henry, the United States had made the decision in favor
of the capitalistic system in 1893, when the financial crisis of
that year had initiated the bitter debate over the gold standard.
For one hundred years the nation had vacillated between the
two forces of simple and finance capitalism. But by 1896 the
decision was final and irrevocable. The results were depressing
for one who still retained memories of a country whose life had
seemed more placid and rewarding. Society, noted Henry
Adams, would now be divided into just two political elements,
the moneylending class and the money-borrowing group.[23]
Nothing could be more cheapening or more deadening, but
there was nothing to do but to accept the inevitable. He deplored what he considered the futile attempts to fight the new
economy. He characterized the Populist movement as a "gro-

---

[23] H. Adams to Charles Milnes Gaskell, April 25, 1895, in Ford, *Letters*,
II, 67.

tesque alliance" of Southern and Western farmers and the city laborers. It stood no chance of success, and he noted that such a combination "had been tried in 1800 and 1828, and had failed even under simple conditions."[24] There was no hope of turning back. The important thing now was to make sure that the capitalists could run the machine they had created. Concerning this, Henry was pessimistic. He believed, as Brooks had indicated, that the United States was in the last stage of concentration. It was possible, he admitted, that further adaptation could be accomplished; but he thought it more likely that the next step would be one of disintegration, with Russia becoming the new challenger.

Both Henry and Brooks Adams foresaw the advent of a more collectivized state as a result of the great increase in the complexities of modern life. Yet the attitudes of each toward such an occurrence differed sharply. Brooks believed that increased governmental control was the only possible solution. America, he argued, would not be able to meet the crises of the twentieth century unless its citizens could be taught the necessity of being able to administer the vast forces now at their disposal. Indeed, one writer has stated that "Brooks Adams was the first American economic historian to occupy himself with the basic problem of our industrial civilization."[25] In other words, Brooks contended that increased collectivism was the one way in which the nation could be saved from aiding in its own destruction.

While Henry could suggest no alternative, he could not agree that with collectivism lay salvation. If anything, he felt, it would mean the death of the individual in America, and it was in the individual that most of the hopes for the fulfillment of the American dream had been placed. He hated to see the best of nineteenth-century liberalism, as personified in the doctrine of John Stuart Mill, collapse and give way to centralized

24 H. Adams, *The Education*, 344.
25 Charles A. Madison, *Critics and Crusaders*, 305.

government. He prophesied that the abandonment of the parliamentary system would be coincidental with social disintegration and that "the despot, the gold-bug, and the anarchists are the real partners in the Trusts of our political future."[26] Bitterly, he announced that he was glad he would be dead before the trade unions assumed control of society. The nation was moving rapidly down the road to consolidation and increased socialism. Henry Adams had little sympathy for either the forces of capital or those of labor. Both had done their share in destroying the beauty and promise that once had been America; both were partly responsible for turning the American dream into a nightmare.

Intimately associated with this national tragedy was the American character, for in the final analysis the defects of any particular society are the failings of its individuals. When such limitations were most conspicuous in the national leadership, there could be little hope for high performances from the rank and file. Henry Adams viewed with both scorn and sympathy the typical American, calling him "bored, patient, helpless; pathetically dependent on his wife and daughters; indulgent to excess; mostly a modest, decent, excellent, valuable citizen." There was nothing vicious in the average American. He was not evil, merely pathetic. He never really looked in a mirror, and if he did, he saw only a national image. "The American thought of himself as a restless, pushing, energetic, ingenious person," when, in reality, he was so ignorant that he had forgotten there was ignorance and did not even understand why he was bored. The great American deficiency, therefore, was the lack of a solid core of values. The average citizen was too smug, too complacent, too superficial to see the real nature of the world about him. Even the shock of the enormous bloodletting of the Civil War had failed to awaken Americans to the omnipresence of tragedy. The country was too busy with its

[26] Letter to Cecil Spring Rice, February 12, 1897, in Ford, *Letters*, II, 122.

"twenty-million-horse power society" to take notice of the "tragic motives that would have overpowered the Middle Ages." The complacent American had an explanation for everything; even death was a neurosis.[27]

Nowhere was the lack of vision and imagination more visible than in the personalities who had dominated political life since 1860. With few exceptions the Adamses excoriated them as an ignoble lot. What was even more appalling was that such men appeared to be characteristic of the nation's intellectual temper. To Henry Adams, who had written eloquently of Albert Gallatin, who had inherited the great dissenting traditions of John Adams and John Quincy Adams, and who had been in government service during the presidency of Abraham Lincoln, the so-called statesmen he saw around him in 1900 were but lower creatures by comparison. The celebrated political management of a Mark Hanna was amateurish when compared to the "benevolent simplicity" and "conquering confidence" of a Thurlow Weed. The presidency, itself, had not had a capable executive since Andrew Johnson, and the United States Senate had deteriorated from the days of William Seward and Stephen A. Douglas to the mediocrity of Roscoe Conkling. A man like Charles Sumner was too ridiculous to be caricatured; he and others like him "were more grotesque than ridicule could make them."[28] Politicians had become the puppets of the vested business interests. They moved only when the strings were pulled, and their words were nothing but meaningless platitudes. The Union had been saved physically at Gettysburg, only to be destroyed spiritually at the White House and on Capitol Hill.

At a more youthful age Henry had had supreme confidence in the ability of America to rebound from any setback and to continue to produce pre-eminent leadership. Even the assassination of Lincoln evoked no cry of despair. In fact, Henry ad-

[27] H. Adams, *Education*, 297, 416.
[28] *Ibid.*, 146, 246, 261.

vised the rest of the nations of the world not to waste pity on the United States. "I am much too strong an American to have thought for a moment that we are going to be shaken by a murder."[29] But a few short years later the Grant era had undermined his previous equanimity. Somewhat jokingly, he noted that the descent from Alexander the Great and Julius Caesar to U. S. Grant made evolution ludicrous. Indeed, "the progress of evolution from President Washington to President Grant, was alone evidence enough to upset Darwin."[30] McKinley, to Henry Adams, was the epitome of the new leadership which neither attracted nor repelled. McKinley, he stated, "will do what his class wants,—no more, no less—and will drift with the world's stream."[31] He was not so sure about the qualifications and abilities of Theodore Roosevelt. Roosevelt seemed to amuse him; Henry could never really consider the Rough Rider seriously. He never became a Roosevelt booster as Brooks did, but at least he found the New Yorker a refreshing change from the seemingly interminable list of mediocrities and nonentities who usually occupied the political spotlight. Nor did Henry find comfort when he looked at the make-up of the Democratic party. That "peerless leader" of the Democracy, William Jennings Bryan, was abruptly dismissed as "a great fool"; but he thought that the rest of the party like "Jones of Arkansas and Gorman and their like" were greater ones, who had made the party nothing more than "a contemptible mob."[32]

Brooks Adams was as chagrined as his brother when he contrasted American leaders of the past with those of his own times. But where Henry had seen no sign of recrudescence, Brooks believed that Theodore Roosevelt might well be the man to

[29] Letter to Charles Milnes Gaskell, April 23, 1865, in *Letters of Henry Adams (1858–1891)*, ed. by Worthington C. Ford, I, 119.

[30] *Education*, 266.

[31] H. Adams to Charles Milnes Gaskell, April 1, 1896, in Ford, *Letters*, II, 104.

[32] H. Adams to Elizabeth Cameron, December 18, 1898, in *ibid.*, II, 196.

rekindle the old flame and once again set a pattern of enlightened leadership. Actually, thought Brooks, the decline had begun when the grandiose concept of Washington had failed. This was the plan, later advanced by Albert Gallatin, of cementing the sections of the new nation together through a system of highways and canals. However, it was not the first president who had failed; rather, it had been the very nature of the democratic process which had been at fault. "Hardly had Washington gone to his grave when the levelling work of the system of averages, on which democracy rests, began."[33] What this nation or any nation demanded was leadership which could transcend the natural processes that inevitably tended toward a tame mediocrity. According to Brooks, this process was well personified in James Madison, who "never had the broad vision that Washington possessed." Madison, he asserted, had created nothing and had represented only the vested interests of Virginia, namely land and slaves.[34] The sinking process then continued to reach a new low when the electorate rejected John Quincy Adams for Andrew Jackson in the election of 1828.

Brooks believed his grandfather to have been capable of providing the nation with the sort of inspirational guidance it so desperately required. Not only was he capable but he was also willing to undertake such a mission. Comparing him to Moses, Brooks declared that "John Quincy Adams had dreamed that, by his interpretation of the divine thought, as manifested in nature, he could covenant with God, and thus regenerate mankind."[35] But his countrymen had refused to allow him such responsibility. They had spurned the man whose ambitious plans for the Union might well have avoided the Civil War.

[33] B. Adams, "Introduction," to H. Adams, *Degradation*, 108.
[34] B. Adams, "Collective Thinking in America," *Yale Review*, Vol. VIII (April, 1919), 626–27.
[35] B. Adams, "Introduction," to H. Adams, *Degradation*, 77.

Instead, said Brooks, they had selected Jackson, who by appointing Roger Taney as Chief Justice of the Supreme Court had sustained the expansion of slavery and made internecine conflict unavoidable. John Quincy Adams, denied the opportunity to save his country, had become a lonely member of the House of Representatives, where he succeeded better in advancing his views than he had done during his four-year tenure as the chief executive. What John Quincy Adams had cherished had been his own version of the American dream.

In twentieth-century United States, Brooks Adams conceived of Theodore Roosevelt as being able to breathe new life into the old dream. Here, perhaps, was a man who understood the forces of history and could accommodate American policy accordingly. As the leader of the Progressive movement, he had foreseen the dangers of an unchained capitalism and had thwarted the masters of finance in their ruinous designs. As a formulator of foreign policy, it was Roosevelt who had detected the drift of civilization that dictated American expansion in the Far East and opposition to the latent enemy, Russia. Undoubtedly, the fact that Roosevelt listened to the advice proffered by Brooks inclined the latter to think highly of Roosevelt's prescience. Nevertheless, there was no hesitancy in Brooks Adams' feeling that finally the country had acquired a leader who would renew the great tradition begun by Washington and which John Quincy Adams had wished to follow. But Roosevelt was only one man. If the dream was to be kept alive, there was need of others.

In addition to a poverty of ideals, a lack of social cohesion, and a deficient leadership, the Adamses attempted to explain the failure of the United States to achieve its potential in terms of its history. Both were convinced that there had been little in American history to warrant optimism concerning the nation's future, although certainly Brooks was the less pessimistic. By comparing their attitudes toward some crucial episodes, it is possible to note that each, however, was somewhat more than dubious that the great American dream would ever be fulfilled.

Henry Adams was perhaps afflicted with what some modern literary critics call the neurosis of the white man's guilt. This thesis holds that throughout American literature there has been a consistent preoccupation with the fate and tragedy of the American Indian. James Fenimore Cooper sought to expiate the sin by making his hero a confidant and friend of Indians. Whether Henry Adams ever consciously felt in such a manner is entirely conjectural, but it can be definitely stated that he believed that the writing of American history must begin with the civilization of the Indian, rather than with the first white settlements.[36] Brooks never expressed himself on the matter, and Henry actually gave little more than lip service to the idea. Yet there is some justification for the assumption that subconsciously most American artists, including Henry Adams, were affected by the guilty knowledge of their white heritage—a heritage which had dictated inhumanity to fellow humans of a different color. In a sense the Negro replaced the Indian on the American scene, and the treatment afforded both cast grave doubts on the realization of the Utopia so often contemplated.

The problem of race was a crucial one in American history, and the great crisis which it engendered was the Civil War. No other event in American history has been so thoroughly analyzed, dramatized, and dissected; yet the war between the states remains somewhat of an enigma. One cannot understand America without having some insight into the great sectional strife of 1861 to 1865; thus, all historians of the United States have been compelled to deal with it in some fashion. Henry and Brooks Adams were no exceptions; each saw it in a different light, but each viewed it as central to the character of the nation.

Henry Adams never quite escaped from the rabid antisecessionist enthusiasm which had come so naturally to him in 1861.

[36] H. Adams to Lewis Henry Morgan, July 14, 1877, in Cater, *Friends*, 83.

In addition to his Puritan New England background, he was actively engaged as a participant as private secretary to his father Charles Francis Adams, who was ambassador to the Court of St. James. Henry had abhorred the indecision of President Buchanan, going so far as to suggest the latter's impeachment. Like many a Northerner, he was convinced that the South was all bluff and that a firm show of strength on the part of the government at Washington would be all that was required to bring the South to heel. He never changed his opinion that the war had been produced by the cotton planters of the South who were ". . . mentally one-sided, ill-balanced, and provincial to a degree rarely known." These men, said Henry, "were stupendously ignorant of the world," and illustrated well the object-lesson of what could happen when an excess of power was held by inadequate hands.[37] His personal presidential choice in 1860 had been William Seward, as he thought the New Yorker to be the only one capable of carrying the nation through without a violent outbreak. But when Lincoln was elected Henry did not feel disappointed, primarily because he believed, as Seward did, that "Seward will be Premier."[38]

To Henry Adams the war was a necessary but incalculable setback to American progress. By creating a spiritual division of the country, it had prevented a united effort directed toward creating a homogeneous and totally progressive culture. The preservation of the Union had been somewhat in the nature of a Pyrrhic victory, for the old American would never return. The real tragedy was that "not one man in America wanted the Civil War." Only a small minority had wanted secession, and nobody had been clever enough to foretell the enormity of the conflict or its dreadful results. With Appomatox the South had been shut away from the mainstream of American life. The

[37] *Education*, 100.
[38] H. Adams to Charles Francis Adams, Jr., November 23, 1859, in Ford, *Letters*, I, 75.

planters had sacrificed the great promise of America on the altar of ". . . bad temper, bad manners, power, and treason."[39]

To Brooks Adams "the Civil War was fought, presumably, to enforce the democratic principle of the natural equality of man."[40] He did not indulge in any complex examination of the infinitely varied facets which contributed to the sectional dilemma. For Brooks the cause of the war had been the desire to extend the basic human rights to the Negro. In essence, therefore, the Civil War had been a fruition of the American dream. For had not the country always been concerned with the preservation and extension of the democratic principle? This had been the chief reason why the Supreme Court had lost the public confidence in the decade of the 1850's. The North found the Dred Scott decision intolerable, not because it violated the spirit of the Constitution, but because it ran counter to the democratic motif. Moreover, the Court had not regained prestige during the war itself because it had sanctioned actions of the Lincoln administration which also damaged the democratic ideal. The Supreme Court, stated Brooks, had injured itself and popular respect for law "far more by its errors, than it aided the Union by its political adjudications."[41] Yet, despite the obvious presence of the democratic dream in the Civil War, Brooks Adams did not believe that the conflict had resulted in any furtherance of that ideal.

The reason that Brooks advanced for such pessimism was based on his consistent contention that there are "fundamental facts which are stronger than democratic theories."[42] The facts of which he spoke were those associated with his law of civilization and decay. The victory of the North in the Civil War had not given to the nation any more real democracy, because the current of history was against it. Democracy assumed an up-

[39] H. Adams, *Education*, 98, 100.
[40] "Introduction," to H. Adams, *Degradation*, vii.
[41] *The Theory of Social Revolutions*, 62.
[42] "Introduction," to H. Adams, *Degradation*, vii.

ward movement—a progressive tendency, while civilization tended downward—a cheapening process. Since the Civil War had been a tremendous stimulant to increased civilization in the form of industrialization and business concentration, the cumulative effect had been one of degradation—not progress. The dream of an ever better America was doomed to failure from the beginning. The Civil War had been the ultimate mockery—an ironic twist in which the goal of equality had been sabotaged by the means used to attain it. The decision had been made for union as opposed to disunion; however, the hope for a better world had not been advanced.

The other period of greatest historical significance to the Adamses was that which began in 1898. Later historians have also subscribed to the theory that the aforementioned date was a turning point in the history of the United States. It was one of those convenient lines of demarcation which seem to divide an older civilization from a newer one. For Americans it was a time when their country seemed to burst with a new energy and to embark once again on an active program in international affairs, the signal for which had been the Spanish-American War. It was also a time which appeared to have ended forever the Jeffersonian dream of a stable agrarian America. By 1898 the nation had obviously embraced industrialism with its attendant virtues and vices. To Henry and Brooks Adams 1898 marked the death of nineteenth-century America both literally and figuratively. However, to Henry this meant the end of the American dream, for its fulfillment was impossible in the brave new world of the twentieth century. To Brooks also the old dream was now impossible, but there was a new challenge for America to face—one which had to be met, not to achieve a Utopia but to survive as a national entity.

Between 1865 and 1898, Henry Adams maintained that the new world had been born. Young men who reached maturity during these years, realizing that they were living during an era of intense change, "could see nothing beyond their day's work." They took an immediate aversion to the antiquated theories that had been abstracted from history, philosophy, and theology. "They knew enough of energies quite new."[43] But by 1908, American society had once again established an equilibrium which Henry satirically described as "the ideal fruit of all our youthful hopes and reforms. Everybody is fairly decent, respectable, domestic, bourgeois, middle-class, and tiresome."[44] The excitement of a dynamic country which had been so prevalent during the first fifty years of the nineteenth-century had been dissipated. In its place was a smug materialism which Henry felt to be completely stultifying. Even the acquisition of a new overseas empire failed to suggest to Henry Adams the recapturing of the old spirit.

Henry had at first greeted the conflict with Spain as ". . . a God-send to all the young men in America." In characteristic fashion he remarked that now "even the Bostonians have at last a chance to show that they have emotions."[45] He had given his approval to the occupation of Asiatic lands, and he spoke in glowing terms of the open-door policy pronounced by his life-long friend John Hay. But as the excitement produced by these momentous events waned, so did Henry's enthusiasm. On more serious reflection he concluded that expansion, while inevitable, simply added more unfamiliar pieces to the American jigsaw puzzle. This, coupled with the tremendous increase in the expenditure of energy, led him to abandon all hope that the American dream could ever be reclaimed. The increased strife between capital and labor seemed to confirm an observation he had made in 1894:

. . . Debs has smashed everything for the present. The working-

[43] H. Adams, *Education*, 239.

[44] Letter to Charles Milnes Gaskell, December 17, 1908, in Ford *Letters*, II, 514.

[45] H. Adams to B. Adams, May 7, 1898, in *ibid.*, II, 178.

man is so brilliant a political failure—so suicidal a political ally, that until he is dead and buried, the gold bug must rule us. George M. Pullman and Andrew Carnegie and Grover Cleveland are our Crassus and Pompey and Caesar,—our proud American triumvirate, the types of our national mind and ideals.[46]

World War I was the finishing stroke to any optimism which Henry might have retained concerning the future of America. The war of 1914–18 was proof to him that his theory of degradation was the correct one. In one of his last prophecies he predicted in 1916 the date that Germany would collapse. His date of August, 1918, was short by only three months. The forecast had been based on the dynamic theory of history which predicted gradual decline rather than progress toward that vague Elysium about which most Americans had dreamed.

Brooks Adams viewed the Spanish-American War and its expansive results as vivid proof of his law of history. He was exhilirated by the demonstration of power. Furthermore, he assumed that the acquisition of lands in Asia was good evidence that the United States had passed a crisis of consolidation successfully. He stated his case thus:

> Competition has entered a period of greater stress; and competition in its acutest form, is war. The present outbreak is, probably, only premonitory; but the prize at stake is now what it has always been in such epochs, the seat of commercial exchanges,—in other words, the seat of empire.[47]

There was not time, he thought, for the United States to concern itself with such sentimental idiocy as the Progressive movement, which had "degenerated into a disintegrating rather than a constructive energy."[48] The impulse toward reform was

[46] Letter to Elizabeth Cameron, July 13, 1894, in *ibid.*, II, 53.

[47] B. Adams, "The Spanish War and the Equilibrium of the World," *Forum*, Vol. XXV (August, 1898), 646.

[48] B. Adams, *The Theory of Social Revolutions*, 5.

wasted effort in a world which could never be reformed. The only question which merited consideration was the elemental one of survival.

Brooks warned his countrymen that the future of the nation lay in its ability to defeat in war a possible coalition of France, Germany, and Russia. The prize over which the conflict would rage was China. It was the key to the future as it contained, according to his cyclical law, the next seat of empire. Consequently, whoever controlled China would dominate the world. Foreign interest, especially Russian, in China boded nothing but trouble for the United States. The more we attempted to develop China economically, the more attractive it would become to other nations. If Russia did not challenge us, then, Brooks deduced, Japan might. He even envisaged the possibility of a Russo-German coalition designed to control China. Any of these events would endanger basic American interests. Consequently, he reasoned that "Americans must accept the Chinese question as the great problem of the future."[49]

The deep tragedy which Henry Adams felt over the passing of the old America was not shared by his brother. Brooks had resigned himself long before to the impossibility of an increased spirituality and moral responsibility. The universe in which his country and her people were contained was neither spiritual nor moral. The only consideration had to be that of survival, and survival depended on applying the national energy and will to things that mattered. There was no sense in wasting them in attempting to fulfill a dream which could never come true.

THE DREAM DISCARDED

The Adamses were undeniably a part of the dream tradition which has consistently found expression not only in literature

[49] B. Adams, "Russia's Interest in China," *Atlantic Monthly*, Vol. LXXXVI (September, 1900), 317; B. Adams, "Introduction," to H. Adams, *Degradation*, 98.

and the arts but in politics as well. Unquestionably, it is likewise true that Henry, more than Brooks, was more overtly concerned with the failure of America to reach the goals her founders had confidently set. But it would be in error to assume that the younger brother was any the less affected. The fierce, almost obsessive love of country which pervades all of the writings of Brooks Adams offers considerable testimony to this fact. With the enunciation of their respective historical laws, both Henry and Brooks Adams had abandoned whatever hopes they held that a thorough searching of historical evidence would lend any support for the dream hypothesis.

The tragedy which Henry Adams saw in American history may well have been a reflection of his own personality. Henry S. Commager believes that Henry summed up the plight of his country. Just as the United States had outgrown provincialism without abandoning her splendid isolation, so Henry Adams had outworn his New England heritage while retaining its psychological chains. The United States had developed an economic machine suitable for the twentieth century but had kept the shibboleths and culture of the eighteenth; Henry had developed an intellect geared to the modern realities of science while holding on to outworn ideals of a dead past. Van Wyck Brooks agrees that the pessimism which Henry exuded concerning the future promise of America was, in fact, a personification of the disillusionment of New England "where faith in the will and progress had once been so strong."[50] The once proud land of the vigorous Puritans and the optimistic transcendentalists had lost its hope and its faith in both the goodness of God and the progress of America. New England took comfort in a theory of gradual degradation of energy because it seemed to explain her own situation.

[50] Henry S. Commager, "Henry Adams," *South Atlantic Quarterly*, Vol. XXVI (July, 1927), 263–64; Van Wyck Brooks, *New England: Indian Summer*, 476–77.

There can be little doubt that Henry Adams represents a great transition in American thought. He was the crucial figure in the abandonment of the old democratic faith of the early nineteenth century. He had laid bare the emptiness and poverty of American life and culture. In this sense his chronological placement should more properly have been in the 1920's, and it was no coincidence that *The Education of Henry Adams* was much more popular with the "lost generation" than it had been a decade earlier. For certainly Henry Adams was a forerunner to T. S. Eliot, F. Scott Fitzgerald, Ernest Hemingway, and Sinclair Lewis. For them as for him the American dream was over. The democratic dream tradition died with Henry Adams, but in its death there were the beginnings of a new and no less vital dream which was geared more to the realities of the modern world. As Ludwig Lewishon expresses it: "Henry Adams is the symbol of the American tradition, hurling itself into the flame of the altar to be consumed so that another tradition . . . might come to be born."[51]

But Henry Adams did not care to take part in preparing the new tradition. For himself the only solution would have been a return to God, in order to replace the shattered complexity of modern existence with the old shining unity. However, this was too much to ask. Like Herman Melville, Henry had quarreled too long with Creation to change. To the end he remained faithful to what he had taught concerning the universe, man, and America: their utter meaninglessness.

It was Brooks Adams who moved boldly forward into the new era and who participated in the formation of a new tradition. It was a tradition which substituted material for spiritual progress and world power for a more perfect democracy. It was not the most attractive of dreams, but it was a dream nonetheless. Brooks declared that "Nature has cast the United States into the vortex of the fiercest struggle which the world has

[51] Ludwig Lewisohn, *Expression in America*, 347.

ever known."[52] In a world of such violent competition the only way for the nation to achieve and maintain supremacy was by wit and force. Otherwise, America would share the fates of other empires which had been roughly discarded by the inexorable motion of history.

Brooks believed that the law which he had discovered made any attempt to retain the old democratic dream a futile one. Instead, his search for a law had convinced him that the United States must concentrate on realizing what nature had intended for her ultimate destiny. This fate, Brooks forecast, was a giant America, "... perched astride of the great trade routes,"[53] dominating human civilization and dictating her commands to a worshipful world. This was the new dream that Americans appeared to embrace as the older and more gentle aspirations slipped unnoticed into oblivion.

[52] *The New Empire*, xxxiv.
[53] B. Adams, "Can War Be Done Away With?" *Papers and Proceedings, American Sociological Society*, Vol. X (1916), 124.

IO.

The Adamses
and American Historiography

THE BREAK WITH THE PAST

THE PUBLICATION OF THE LAWS OF Henry and Brooks Adams
at the turn of the century constituted a definite break in the
chain of American historiography, and the writing of history
in this country would never quite be the same when the links
were reforged. The romantic and nationalistic school of history
which had been fading for twenty-five years was given a shattering blow, and the scientific school which had risen to prominence during the same time was forced to take a closer look at
purposes and goals and to pay less attention to method.

The writing of strictly romantic history now was relegated
to the amateur or the popularizer. For by attempting to give
history laws, the Adamses had pointed out the vitality and intrinsic meaningfulness of the study of history. They had shown
that history and man and man's fate were inextricably interlaced. Certainly, any discipline which had as its major concern
these basic problems of human existence was worthy of the
most serious study. History might well be a humanity rather
than a science; it might well be literature as well as knowledge.
But it also was more. It represented a valid attempt on the part
of man to understand both himself and the society in which he
lived. Undoubtedly, romantic histories like those of Francis

The Adamses and American Historiography

Parkman or William Prescott contained much valid history and much attractive writing, but their appeal was directed toward an audience whose interest was particular and antiquarian. Henry and Brooks Adams were writing for the more limited group whose interest was objective and educational. The romantics had performed a service by offering momentary escape to a past peopled by heroes; the Adamses offered schemes of history to explain the crushing complexities of reality. History, they felt, should not be a method of liberation from an unpleasant present but should be one means by which that present could be better understood.

In understanding the present the Adamses also contributed a devastating criticism to that school of American historiography which had glorified America by extolling its virtues and ignoring its limitations. These ideas had been best personified in the writings of George Bancroft, although many historians had written in the same nationalistic spirit. Henry and Brooks Adams had demonstrated the fallacy of such an approach in two significant ways. First, they had shown the necessity of looking at history from a universal or world viewpoint. All events in history were interrelated, and to treat a national history as a complete and independent entity was distortion. America was a part of an organic complex, and while she might have a unique cultural milieu, United States history could neither be explained nor understood within a strict national framework. Secondly, the Adamses had probed deeply into the deficiencies of American life. What they had uncovered did not warrant an uncritical optimism. They warned that the veneration of nineteenth-century political and social ideals might easily lead to calamity, for in the twentieth century the "historic American political model was inadequate to the task of administering the conflict of new forces."[1] Both brothers were

[1] Richard P. Blackmur, "Henry Adams and Brooks Adams: Parallel to Two Generations," *Southern Review*, Vol. V (1939), 325.

deeply concerned with the apparent apathy with which Americans regarded their current problems, and they contended that history written so as to make citizens more comfortable in their delusions was delinquent in its scholarly duty. After 1900 the publication of purely nationalist-oriented history declined in America, and the Adamses had to some degree influenced this development.

Their impact on the writing of scientific history was also considerable, if more difficult to evaluate precisely. What first must be made clear is a definition of terms. The term "scientific history," as usually employed, refers to the practice and method of writing history. It infers that the historical method as perfected in Germany by Leopold von Ranke and subsequently introduced in American universities should be based upon the approved scientific practices of observation and experiment. Furthermore, it is predicated on the assumption that through strict objectivity, impartiality, and a dependence on primary source materials, the historian will be able to present a reasonably accurate reconstruction of the past. Indeed, this was the ideal to which Henry Adams was originally dedicated; his studies of Anglo-Saxon institutions and his history of the Jefferson and Madison eras were examples of history written along these lines. There is, however, another meaning to "scientific history" to which both Henry and Brooks Adams later subscribed. This second definition asserts that history, in truth, is a science and is consequently subject to natural laws in its operation in the same fashion as the natural and physical sciences. This idea, then, goes much farther than the first. It is more than a simple application of the scientific method; it is an affirmation of the possibility of exact calculation. This was what Brooks Adams had in mind when he pleaded for scientific history. This was what he and his brother attempted to write.

After Henry and Brooks had made their search for a law, the school of scientific history was forced to admit the essential duality inherent in their philosophy. There was a forced recognition that a distinction existed between science and the scientific method. The Adamses had pointed to the patent absurdity that history could claim to be a science simply because historians adopted the technique of science. If history was ever to achieve a status comparable to physics or mathematics, then it would have to formulate hypotheses and laws in a similar manner.

Only a few leading American historians since 1900 have attempted with any serious intentions to pursue the objectives which Henry and Brooks Adams had outlined. To many the feeling that historical laws were impossible to ascertain was insistent enough to prevent scholarly work directed to such ends. But those who turned their back on any identification of history as science also had to drop the title of "scientific history" as a meaningful term. Indeed, at the present time the term is seldom employed except to describe generally that period in American historiography from 1875 to 1900. Most members of the profession today prefer to see history as combining the method of science with the spirit of the humanities. If the Adamses performed no other service for the writing of history, they forced historians to come to terms with the nature of their vocation and to make conscious decisions about what should be the purpose of their work. It was perhaps a negative effect, for, in general, practicing historians in the United States have rejected the plea for a truly scientific history.[2]

Some significant exceptions to this general trend should be noted. Edward P. Cheyney in his presidential message of 1923 to the American Historical Association stressed the importance of laws in history and maintained that they were self-evident. He cited six laws which he, himself, had found to be operative throughout history.[3] Henry Osborn Taylor urged his col-

[2] For an excellent discussion of this rejection and the major motive behind it, consult Herman Ausubel, *Historians and Their Craft*, 221-55.

[3] "Law in History," *American Historical Review*, Vol. XXIX (January, 1924), 231-48.

leagues in the historical profession to search out the unknown in history and to discover the laws which governed historical movement.[4] The most notable pronouncement was made by Charles A. Beard, who urged his fellow historians to find the appropriate measuring sticks for history; he deplored the appropriation of the laws of the physical and natural sciences and believed that the historian must improvise his own method of calculation. But he did assert that a scientific history was possible.[5] Yet Cheyney, Taylor, and Beard were not typical. Most of their colleagues preferred to disregard the challenge of writing scientific history, not only because it seemed absurd but also because it would inevitably introduce the crucial problem of historical philosophy. The discovery of historical laws would, of necessity, require answers to the problem of meaning in history. American historians have preferred to leave such quests to the Toynbees of the world. While this is by far the safer course, there remains considerable doubt that it is the most courageous. The ancient advice of Plato to "Know thyself" may be ignored by historians but only at the risk of denying a solemn responsibility.

A FINAL EVALUATION

It would be pleasant to conclude by arguing that Henry Adams and Brooks Adams stand as overwhelming giants in historiography and that their influence on the writing of history can be detected everywhere. But this is not the case. The Adamses did leave an imprint on both history and historians; however, their mark was neither indelible nor all pervasive. Certainly, some of the ideas which they considered important have continued to be influential in directing the investigations

[4] Henry Osborn Taylor, "A Layman's View of History," *American Historical Review,* Vol. XXXIII (January, 1928), 247–56.

[5] Charles A. Beard, "Written History as an Act of Faith," *American Historical Review,* Vol. XXXIX (January,1934), 219–29.

of historians. Of these ideas at least five are significant enough to merit mention.

The stress which both Henry and Brooks placed on the necessity for history to be meaningful in the contemporary world was undeniably a factor in the relativist movement pioneered by Carl Becker and James H. Robinson. The emphasis given, especially by Henry Adams, to the significance of ideas in human development was likewise a decisive argument for the exponents of Robinson's "new history," and a starting point for the study of intellectual history which only now is acquiring stature as a legitimate field for historical endeavor. Another thought awarded great importance by the Adamses was that historians must not be afraid to use all available tools in their research. The use which Henry made of the principles of physics and that which Brooks made of Darwinian and economic axioms offer ample proof that each was willing to break new ground. This feeling was most recently manifested when William D. Langer strongly advocated to members of the American Historical Association that the insights and techniques of modern psychiatry should be fully exploited by historians.[6] The Adamses also contended in theory and themselves practiced the idea that all parts of the past may be relevant to the present. What happened in ancient Egypt may be as vital to contemporary society as what occurred last year. This idea has recently received additional support from Geoffrey Barraclough.[7] Finally, the notion that the historian must relate his findings to the entire philosophical and cultural structure has received increasing approval from members of the historical profession.

Regardless of the specific contributions made by the Adamses to the ideas of history, their most dramatic impact was personal

[6] William D. Langer, "The Next Assignment," *American Historical Review*, Vol. LXIII (January, 1958), 283–304.
[7] Geoffrey Barraclough, *History in a Changing World*, 1–30.

and emotional. Any final evaluation must concern itself with their intense personalities, for this is what one remembers. It was not so much what they wrote and said but what they were that captures the imagination and makes Henry and Brooks Adams memorable descendants of one of the nation's proudest families. It was their vitality as human beings which impresses the mind; their ability to ensnare the universal and to see the whole of human society is the compelling factor in their fascination. each accomplished this in a different and characteristic manner despite the close ties of blood, interests, and a shared belief in the possibility of ascertaining historical laws.

Henry Adams approached life obliquely. He preferred to attack a problem from the flank and to obscure his real intentions with a subtlety and ironic humor that characterized both his conversation and his writings. He was a peripatetic seeker after knowledge, and he usually had a certain amount of sound information on almost any subject.[8] Undeniably, his rather elliptical method was the mask he adopted to disguise the deep concern he felt for the world in which he lived. To dismiss Henry Adams as being simply quixotic would be to lose the true meaning of his character. His search for unity in a universe of complexity was as serious and desperate as the world has seen. Moreover, he made the search "in the face of betrayal without and distrust within himself."[9] His brother Brooks was always aware of Henry's profound desire to find an affirmation in religion, history, or science for all of the old values. He knew how deeply the disillusionment had penetrated and noted that "Mr. Adams always adored order and loathed the very idea of chaos. Yet he died for astronomy, the science of chaos."[10]

Reluctantly, Henry Adams had forsaken the Middle Ages. It had been the one period in Western history when there had

[8] Cater, *Friends*, lxxxiii.

[9] Robert M. Lovett, "The Betrayal of Henry Adams," *Dial*, Vol. LXV (November 30, 1918), 472.

[10] B. Adams, "Introduction," to H. Adams, *Degradation*, 122.

seemed to be any real unity. That had been the time when "the hive of Saint Thomas sheltered God and man, mind and matter, the universe and the atom, within the walls of a harmonious home."[11] Denied the harbor of such a home, Henry had sought safety in science. Once more he was turned away. The stars as well as man were dying vestiges of depleted energy. History was a sham which offered no hope for a future dynamism. To cushion this crushing revelation, he retreated once again into a protective shell of indifference:

> As I grow old, I grow tall in the sense of growing unpractical. I see in history two social attitudes, the one, that of motion, the other that of station. Between them, I care little to choose.[12]

Brooks Adams also reacted to the chaos of the modern world; but whereas Henry was ever subtle and paradoxical, the younger brother preferred the frontal attack. By nature an argumentative and erratic personality, Brooks responded by demonstrating the logic of history—"that the new centralization was self-destructive and represented civilization in an advanced state of decay."[13] He made no concession to sentimentality, but an assumed indifference was beyond his capacity. If the world was governed by harsh and immutable law, unameliorated by the hope of divine mercy, then Brooks Adams was willing to live within those laws. Moreover, he intended that man, tragic as his eventual fate might be, should seek to take advantage of those laws and continue the fight. There is always something of the fierce will to survive in him. If Henry personifies man as the rational animal, Brooks typifies the human will. He glorified the combative instinct; man could stand up and fight for the fullness of life. He could not be flippant about the impend-

---

11 H. Adams, *Mont-Saint-Michel*, 388.
12 H. Adams to B. Adams, September 22, 1913, in Cater, *Friends*, 758.
13 Blackmur, "Henry Adams and Brooks Adams," *Southern Review*, Vol. V (1939), 313.

ing doom. Although Brooks made a great pretense at being fatalistic, he did not enjoy himself. Daniel Aaron feels that ". . . behind the façade of scientific detachment can be discerned a prevailing sympathy for man in his uneven contest with nature."[14]

The searching was over. Henry and Brooks Adams had presented a system of laws for future generations of historians to ponder, to dissect, to refute. They had earned permanent niches in the often dusty annals of American historiography. But their right to occupy such stations rests not alone on solid scholarship and creative minds. The Adamses had responded to those impulses which spring from the more noble of human aspirations—those which still offer some hope that man can someday realize the potentiality for greatness he instinctively feels possible. The achievement of Henry and Brooks Adams does not stem from their formulation of exact historical laws, for in that they were failures. The glory of the Adamses lies in the fact that they ventured on the eternal quest for the meaning and significance of life. Surely, for the historian there can be no higher calling.

[14] Brooks Adams: The Unusable Man," *New England Quarterly*, Vol. XXI (March, 1948), 33.

Bibliography

I. WRITINGS OF HENRY ADAMS

1. *Books*

Adams, Henry. *The Degradation of the Democratic Dogma.* Introduction by Brooks Adams. Capricorn Edition. New York, G. P. Putnam's Sons, 1958.

———. *Democracy: An American Novel.* New York, Henry Holt and Co., 1880.

———, ed. *Documents Relating to New England Federalism, 1800-1815.* Boston, Little, Brown & Co., 1877.

———. *The Education of Henry Adams.* New York, The Modern Library, 1931.

———. *Esther: A Novel.* New York, Henry Holt and Co., 1884.

———. *The Great Secession Winter and Other Essays.* Edited and with an introduction by George Hockfield. New York, Sagamore Press, 1958.

———. *A Henry Adams Reader.* Edited and with an introduction by Elizabeth Stevenson. Garden City, Doubleday and Co., 1959.

———. *Historical Essays.* New York, Charles Scribner's Sons, 1891.

———. *History of the United States of America During the Administrations of Jefferson and Madison.* 9 vols. New York, Charles Scribner's Sons, 1889-91.

———. *John Randolph.* "American Statesmen Series." Boston, Houghton Mifflin Co., 1898.

———. *The Life of Albert Gallatin.* Philadelphia, J. B. Lippincott Co., 1879.

———. *The Life of George Cabot Lodge.* Boston, Houghton Mifflin Co., 1911.

———. *Mont-Saint-Michel and Chartres.* Anchor Edition. Garden City, Doubleday and Co., 1959.

2. *Articles*

Adams, Henry. "American Finance, 1865–1869," *Edinburgh Review,* Vol. CXXIX (April, 1869), 504–33.

———. "The Bank of England Restriction," *North American Review,* Vol. CV (October, 1867), 393–434.

———. "British Finance in 1816," *North American Review,* Vol. CIV (April, 1867), 354–86.

———. "Captaine John Smith," *North American Review,* Vol. CIV (January, 1867), 1–30.

———. "Civil Service Reform," *North American Review,* Vol. CIX (October, 1869), 443–76.

———. "Count Edward de Crillon," *American Historical Review,* Vol. I (October, 1895), 51–69.

———. "The New York Gold Conspiracy," *Westminster Review,* Vol. XXXVIII (October, 1870), 411–36.

———. "The Quincy Memoirs and Speeches," *North American Review,* Vol. CXX (January, 1875), 235–36.

———. "Saturday Review Sketches and Essays," *North American Review,* Vol. CXVIII (April, 1874), 401–405.

———. "The Session, 1869–1870," *North American Review,* Vol. CXI (July, 1870), 29–62.

———. "Washington in 1861," *Proceedings, Massachusetts Historical Society,* Vol. XLIII (June, 1910), 656–89.

Adams, Henry, and Charles F. Adams, Jr. "The Independents in the Canvass," *North American Review,* Vol. CXXIII (October, 1876), 426–67.

Adams, Henry, and Francis A. Walker. "The Legal Tender Act," *North American Review,* Vol. CX (April, 1870), 299–327.

3. *Correspondence*

Adams, Henry. *Henry Adams and His Friends: A Collection of His Unpublished Letters.* Edited by Harold D. Cater. New York, Macmillan Co., 1947.

———. *Letters of Henry Adams, 1858–91.* Edited by Worthington C. Ford. [I]. Boston and New York. Houghton Mifflin Co., 1930.

———. *Letters of Henry Adams, 1892–1918.* Edited by Worthington C. Ford. [II]. Boston and New York, Houghton Mifflin Co., 1938.

Cater, Harold D. See Adams, Henry.

Cook, Albert S., ed. "Six Letters of Henry Adams," *Yale Review,* Vol. X (October, 1920), 131–40.

———. "Three Letters of Henry Adams," *Pacific Review,* Vol. II (September, 1921), 273–75.

Davis, Edward H., ed. "Letters and Comment," *Yale Review,* Vol. XI (October, 1921), 218–21.

Ford, Worthington S. See Adams, Henry.

Laski, Harold J., ed. "Henry Adams: An Unpublished Letter," *Nation,* Vol. CLI (August 3, 1940), 94–95.

Leslie, Shane, ed. "Letters of Henry Adams," *Yale Review,* Vol. XXIV (September, 1934), 112–17.

Luquiens, Frederick Bliss, ed. "Seventeen Letters of Henry Adams," *Yale Review,* Vol. X (October, 1920), 111–40.

4. *Book Reviews*

Adams, Henry. Review of *The Administration of Andrew Jackson* by Hermann von Holst. *North American Review,* Vol. CXX (January, 1875), 179–85.

———. Review of *The Ancient City* by Fusted de Coulanges. *North American Review,* Vol. CXVIII (April, 1874), 390–97.

———. Review of *The Building of a Brain* by E. H. Clarke. *North American Review,* Vol. CXX, (January, 1875), 185–88.

———. Review of *The Early History of Institutions* by Sir Henry Maine. *North American Review,* Vol. CXX (April, 1875), 432–38.

———. Review of *Historical Essays* by E. A. Freeman. *North American Review,* Vol. CXIV (January, 1872), 193–96.

——. Review of *History of the Norman Conquest* by E. A. Freeman. *North American Review*, Vol. CXVIII (January, 1874), 176–81.

——. Review of *History of the United States* by George Bancroft. *North American Review*, Vol. CXX (April, 1875), 424–32.

——. Review of *Letters and Other Writings of the late Edward Denison* edited by Sir Baldwyn Leighton. *North American Review*, Vol. CXIV (April, 1872), 426–32.

——. Review of *Mountaineering in the Sierra Nevada* by Henry King. *North American Review*, Vol. CXIV (April, 1872), 445–48.

——. Review of *The Old Regime in Canada* by Francis Parkman. *North American Review*, Vol. CXX (January, 1875), 175–79.

——. Review of *Poems* by Francis Turner Palgrave. *North American Review*, Vol. CXX (April, 1874), 438–44.

——. Review of *Principles of Geology* by Sir Charles Lyell. *North American Review*, Vol. CVII (October, 1868), 465–501.

——. Review of *Procedure de la Lex Salica* by R. Sohm. *North American Review*, Vol. CXVIII (April, 1874), 416–25.

——. Review of *Recollections of Past Life* by Sir Henry Holland. *North American Review*, Vol. CXIV (April, 1872), 448–50.

——. Review of *Their Wedding Journey* by William D. Howells. *North American Review*, Vol. CXIV (April, 1872), 444–45.

——. Review of *Village Communities* by Sir Henry Maine. *North American Review*, Vol. CXIV (January, 1872), 196–99.

Adams, Henry, and Henry Lodge. Review of *History of the United States* by Hermann von Holst. *North American Review*, Vol. CXXIII (October, 1876), 328–61.

II. WRITINGS OF BROOKS ADAMS

1. *Books*

Adams, Brooks. *America's Economic Supremacy*. Edited by Marquis Childs. Revised Edition. New York, Macmillan Co., 1947.

——. "Introduction," to Henry Adams, *The Degradation of the Democratic Dogma*. Capricorn Edition. New York, G. P. Putnam's Sons, 1958.

———. *The Emancipation of Massachusetts: The Dream and the Reality*. Boston, Houghton Mifflin Co., 1919.

———. *The Law of Civilization and Decay: An Essay on History*. With an introduction by Charles A. Beard. Vintage Edition. New York, Alfred A. Knopf, Inc., 1955.

———. *The New Empire*. New York, Macmillan Co., 1902.

———. *The Theory of Social Revolutions*. New York, Macmillan Co., 1913.

2. *Articles*

Adams, Brooks. "Abuse of Taxation," *Atlantic Monthly*, Vol. XLII (October, 1878), 453–58.

———. "Advance in the Arts as a Restraint Upon Waste," *American Architect*, Vol. LXXIV (December, 1901), 99–100.

———. "The American Democratic Ideal," *Yale Review*, Vol. V (January, 1916), 225–33.

———. "Can War Be Done Away With," *Papers and Proceedings, American Sociological Society*, Vol. X (1916), 103–24.

———. "The Collapse of Capitalistic Government," *Atlantic Monthly*, Vol. CXI (April, 1913), 433–43.

———. "Collective Thinking in America," *Yale Review*, Vol. VIII (April, 1919), 623–40.

———. "The Consolidation of Colonies," *Atlantic Monthly*, Vol. LV (March, 1885), 302–308.

———. "The Convention of 1800 with France," *Proceedings, Massachusetts Historical Society*, Vol. XLIV (February, 1911), 377–428.

———. "Economic Conditions for Future Defense," *Atlantic Monthly*, Vol. XCII (November, 1903), 632–49.

———. "The Embryo of a Commonwealth," *Atlantic Monthly*, Vol. LIV (November, 1884), 610–19.

———. "England's Decadence in the West Indies," *Forum*, Vol. XXVII (June, 1899), 464–78.

———. "The Gold Standard: An Historical Study," *Fortnightly Review*, Vol. LXII (August, 1894), 242–62.

———. "John Hay," *McClure's Magazine*, Vol. XIX (June, 1902), 173–82.

——. "The Kimpton Case," *Nation*, Vol. XXVII (September 12, 1878), 162–63.

——. "The Last State of English Whiggery," *Atlantic Monthly*, Vol. XLVII (April, 1881), 567–72.

——. "Legal Supervision of the Transportation Tax," *North American Review*, Vol. CLXXIX (September, 1904), 371–87.

——. "Mrs. John Quincy Adams' Narrative of a Journey from St. Petersburg to Paris," *Scribner's Magazine*, Vol. XXXIV (October, 1903), 449–63.

——. "Natural Selection in Literature," *Anglo-Saxon*, Vol. II (September, 1899), 158–80.

——. "The New Departure in Public Schools," *Atlantic Monthly*, Vol. XLV (March, 1880), 408–12.

——. "The New Industrial Revolution," *Atlantic Monthly*, Vol. LXXXVII (February, 1901), 157–65.

——. "The New Struggle for Life among Nations," *Fortnightly Review*, Vol. LXXI (February, 1899), 274–83. Revised and reprinted in *McClure's Magazine*, Vol. XII (April, 1899), 558–64.

——. "Oppressive Taxation and Its Remedy," *Atlantic Monthly*, Vol. XLII (November, 1878), 761–68.

——. "Oppressive Taxation of the Poor," *Atlantic Monthly*, Vol. XLII (November, 1878), 623–36.

——. "The Platform of the New Party," *North American Review*, Vol. CXIX (July, 1874), 33–60.

——. "A Problem in Civilization," *Atlantic Monthly*, Vol. CVI (July, 1910), 26–32.

——. "Reciprocity or the Alternative," *Atlantic Monthly*, Vol. LXXXVIII (August, 1901), 145–55.

——. "The Revolt of Modern Democracy Against Standards of Duty," *Proceedings, American Academy of Arts and Letters*, Vol. IX (November, 1916), 8–12.

——. "Russia's Interest in China," *Atlantic Monthly*, Vol. LXXXVI (September, 1900), 309–17.

——. "The Seizure of the Laird Rams," *Proceedings, Massachusetts Historical Society*, Vol. XLV (December, 1911), 242–333.

——. "The Spanish War and the Equilibrium of the World," *Forum*, Vol. XXV (August, 1898), 641–51.

———. "The Supreme Court and the Currency Question," *International Review*, Vol. VI (June, 1879), 635–49.

———. "Taxation of Interstate Commerce," *International Review*, Vol. X (May, 1881), 428–36.

———. "War and Economic Competition," *Scribner's Magazine*, Vol. XXXI (March, 1902), 344–52.

3. *Book Reviews*

Adams, Brooks. Review of *Fears from the American Point of View for Democracy* by Charles Ingersoll. *North American Review*, Vol. CXXI (July, 1875), 224–28.

———. Review of *Liberty, Equality, Fraternity* by James Fitzjames Stephen. *North America Review*, Vol. CXVIII (April, 1874), 444–47.

———. Review of *The Undiscovered Country* by William D. Howells. *International Review*, Vol. IX (August, 1880), 149–54.

III. SECONDARY MATERIAL: HENRY ADAMS

1. *Books*

Adams, James Truslow. *Henry Adams and the Adams Family*. New York, Albert and Charles Boni, Inc., 1933.

———. Chap. IV, Part III, *The Tempo of Modern Life*. New York, Albert and Charles Boni, Inc., 1931.

Bassett, John S. "Later Historians," in *Cambridge History of American Literature*, III. New York, Macmillan Co., 1921.

Baym, Max I. *The French Education of Henry Adams*. New York, Columbia University Press, 1951.

Beach, Joseph W. "Henry Adams," in *The Outlook for American Prose*. Chicago, University of Chicago Press, 1926.

Becker, Carl. *Detachment and the Writing of History: Essays and Letters of Carl L. Becker*. Edited by Phil L. Snyder. Ithaca, Cornell University Press, 1958.

———. *Everyman His Own Historian*. New York, Crofts and Co., 1935.

Commager, Henry S. Chap. X, in William T. Hutchinson (ed.),

The Marcus Jernegan Essays in American Historiography. Chicago, University of Chicago Press, 1937.

Cournos, John. "Henry Adams: Another Failure," in *A Modern Plutarch.* Indianapolis, Bobbs-Merrill Co., 1928.

Hume, Robert A. *Henry Adams: A Runaway Star.* Ithaca, Cornell University Press, 1951.

Jordy, William H. *Henry Adams: Scientific Historian.* New Haven, Yale University Press, 1952.

Kronenberger, Louis. Chap. II, in Malcom Cowley and Bernard Smith (eds.), *Brooks That Changed Our Minds.* New York, Doubleday, Doran, and Co., 1939.

More, Paul E. "Henry Adams," in *A New England Group and Others.* "*Shelburne Essays,*" 11th Series. Boston and New York, Houghton Mifflin Co., 1921.

Rukeyser, Muriel. *Willard Gibbs.* Garden City, Doubleday, Doran, and Co., 1942.

Samuels, Ernest. *Henry Adams: The Middle Years.* Cambridge, Massachusetts, Harvard University Press, 1958.

———. *The Young Henry Adams.* Cambridge, Massachusetts, Harvard University Press, 1948.

Schevill, Ferdinand. *Six Historians.* Chicago, University of Chicago Press, 1956.

Schneider, Herbert W. *A History of American Philosophy.* New York, Columbia University Press, 1946.

Shafer, Robert. *Progress and Science.* New Haven, Yale University Press, 1922.

Slochower, Harry. "Henry Adams and T. S. Eliot on Unity," in *No Voice Is Wholly Lost.* New York, Creative Age Press, Inc., 1945.

Spiller, Robert E. Chap. LXV, in Robert E. Spiller and others, *Literary History of the United States,* II. New York, Macmillan Co., 1948.

Stevenson, Elizabeth. *Henry Adams: A Biography.* New York, Macmillan Co., 1956.

White, Leslie. "Energy and the Development of Civilization," in Warren Weaver (ed.), *The Scientists Speak.* New York, Boni and Gaer, Inc., 1947.

2. *Articles*

Basso, Hamilton. "A Mind in the Making," *New Yorker*, Vol. XXIII (March 29, 1947), 103–106.

Baym, Max I. "Henry Adams and His Critics," *American Scholar*, Vol. XV (Winter, 1945–46), 79–89.

——. "Henry Adams and Henry Vignaud," *New England Quarterly*, Vol. XVII (September, 1944), 442–49.

——. "William James and Henry Adams," *New England Quarterly*, Vol. X (December, 1937), 717–42.

Blackmur, Richard P. "The Expense of Greatness: Three Emphases on Henry Adams," *Virginia Quarterly Review*, Vol. XII (July, 1936), 396–415.

——. "Henry Adams and Brooks Adams: Parallel to Two Generations," *Southern Review*, Vol. V (1939), 308–34.

——. "Henry Adams: Three Late Moments," *Kenyon Review*, Vol. II (Winter, 1940), 7–29.

Blunt, Hugh F. "The Mal-Education of Henry Adams," *Catholic World*, Vol. CXLV (April, 1937), 46–52.

Commager, Henry S. "Henry Adams," *South Atlantic Quarterly*, Vol. XXVI (July, 1927), 252–65.

——. "Henry Adams, Prophet of our Disjointed World," *New New York Times Magazine* (February 20, 1938), 11.

Creek, Herbert L. "The Medievalism of Henry Adams," *South Atlantic Quarterly*, Vol. XXIV (January, 1925), 86–97.

Delany, Seldon P. "Man of Mystery," *North American Review*, Vol. CCXVI (November, 1922), 694–704.

Dunning, William A. "Henry Adams on Things in General," *Political Science Quarterly*, Vol. XXXIV (June, 1919), 305–11.

Edwards, Herbert. "Henry Adams: Political and Statesman," *New England Quarterly*, Vol. XXII (March, 1949), 49–60.

——. "The Prophetic Mind of Henry Adams," *College English*, Vol. III (May, 1942), 708–21.

Glicksberg, Charles I. "Henry Adams and the Repudiation of Science," *Scientific Monthly*, Vol. LXIV (January, 1947), 63–71

Howe, Mark A. D. "Elusive Henry Adams," *Saturday Review of Literature*, Vol. VII (October 18, 1930), 237.

Jordy, William H. "Henry Adams and Walt Whitman," *South Atlantic Quarterly*, Vol. XL (April, 1941), 132–45.

Kronenberger, Louis. "The Education of Henry Adams," *New Republic*, Vol. XCVIII (March 15, 1939), 155–58.

Lovett, Robert M. "The Betrayal of Henry Adams," *Dial*, Vol. LXV (November 30, 1918), 468–72.

Lydenberg, John. "Henry Adams and Lincoln Steffens," *South Atlantic Quarterly*, Vol. XLVIII (January, 1949), 42–64.

Mumford, Howard M. "The Tendency of History," *New England Quarterly*, Vol. XXXII (March, 1959), 79–90.

Neufeld, Maurice F. "Crisis in Prospect: Henry Adams and the White City," *American Scholar*, Vol. IV (Autumn, 1935), 397–408.

Nichols, Roy F. "The Dynamic Interpretation of History," *New England Quarterly*, Vol. VIII (June, 1935), 163–78.

Quinlivian, Frances. "Irregularities in the Mental Mirror," *Catholic World*, Vol. CXLIII (April, 1946), 58–65.

Roelfos, Gerrit H. "Henry Adams: Pessimism and the Intelligent Use of Doom," *Journal of English Literary History*, Vol. XVII (September, 1950), 214–39.

Schlesinger, Arthur M., Jr. "The Other Henry Adams," *Nation*, Vol. CLXVII (December 25, 1948), 727.

Shepard, Odell. "The Ghost of Henry Adams," *Nation*, Vol. CXLVII (October 22, 1938), 419.

Shumate, Roger V. "Political Philosophy of Henry Adams," *American Political Science Review*, Vol. XVIII (August, 1934), 599–610.

Spiller, Robert E. "Henry Adams: Man of Letters," *Saturday Review of Literature*, Vol. XXX (February 22, 1947), 11.

Stone, James. "Henry Adams' Philosophy of History," *New England Quarterly*, Vol. XIV (September, 1941), 538–48.

Taylor, William R. "Historical Bifocals on the Year 1800," *New England Quarterly* Vol. XXIII (June, 1950), 172–86.

Wecter, Dixon. "The Harvard Exiles," *Virginia Quarterly Review*, Vol. X (April, 1934), 244–57.

Wright, Nathalia. "Henry Adams' Theory of History: A Puritan

Bibliography

Defense," *New England Quarterly*, Vol. XVIII (June, 1945), 204–10.

IV. SECONDARY MATERIAL: BROOKS ADAMS

1. *Books*

Aaron, Daniel. *Men of Good Hope: A Study of American Progressives*. New York, Oxford University Press, 1951.

Amory, Cleveland. *The Proper Bostonians*. New York, E. P. Dutton & Co., 1947.

Anderson, Thornton. *Brooks Adams: Cautious Conservative*. Ithaca, Cornell University Press, 1951.

Barnes, Harry E. *Historical Sociology: Its Origins and Development*. New York, Philosophical Library, Inc., 1948.

Beringause, Arthur F. *Brooks Adams: A Biography*. New York, Alfred A. Knopf, Inc., 1955.

Dorfman, Joseph. *The Economic Mind In American Civilization*, III. New York, Viking Press, Inc., 1949.

Josephson, Matthew. *The President-Makers*. New York, Harcourt, Brace and Co., 1940.

Madison, Charles A. *Critics and Crusaders*. New York, Henry Holt and Co., 1947.

Seligman, Edwin R. A. *The Economic Interpretation of History*. New York, Columbia University Press, 1907.

Wector, Dixon. *The Saga of American Society*. New York, Charles Scribner's Sons, 1937.

2. *Articles*

Aaron, Daniel. "Brooks Adams: The Unusable Man," *New England Quarterly*, Vol. XXI (March, 1948), 3–33.

Baldwin, Summerfield. "Brooks Adams," *Commonweal*, Vol. V (March 16, 1927), 519–20.

Barnes, Harry E. "Brooks Adams on World Utopias," *Current History*, Vol. VI (January, 1944), 1–6.

Chamberlain, John. "In Brooks Adams' Crystal Ball," *New York Times Book Review* (October 12, 1947), 6.

Ford, Worthington C. "Memoir of Brooks Adams," *Proceedings, Massachusetts Historical Society*, Vol. LX (May, 1927), 345–58.

Hudson, Adelbert L. "Equality before the Law," *Atlantic Monthly*, Vol. CXII (November, 1913), 679–88.

Madison, Charles A. "Brooks Adams, Caustic Cassandra," *American Scholar*, Vol. IX (April, 1940), 214–27.

Sargent, Leonard. "An Adams in a Monastery," *Commonweal*, Vol. XIII (December 10, 1930), 156–57.

Williams, William A. "Brooks Adams and American Expansion," *New England Quarterly*, Vol. XXV (June, 1952), 217–32.

3. Book Reviews

Adams, George B. Review of *The Law of Civilization and Decay* by Brooks Adams. *Yale Review*, Vol. IV (February, 1896), 451–53.

Anon. Review of *America's Economic Supremacy* by Brooks Adams. *Literary Digest*, Vol. XXI (November 24, 1900), 611–12.

———. Review of *America's Economic Supremacy* by Brooks Adams. *Yale Review*, Vol. IX (November, 1900), 359.

———. Review of *The Emancipation of Massachusetts* by Brooks Adams. *American Historical Review*, Vol. XXV (January, 1920), 325–26.

———. Review of *The Emancipation of Massachusetts* by Brooks Adams. *Dial*, Vol. VII (March, 1887), 263–68.

———. Review of *The Emancipation of Massachusetts* by Brooks Adams. *Nation*, Vol. XLIV (March 3, 1887), 189–90.

———. Review of *The Emancipation of Massachusetts* by Brooks Adams. *Nation*, Vol. CIX (December 6, 1919), 721.

———. Review of *The Emancipation of Massachusetts* by Brooks Adams. *New York Times Book Review*, Vol. XXIV (October 26, 1919), 594.

———. Review of *The Emancipation of Massachusetts* by Brooks Adams. *Outlook*, Vol. CXXIII (December 3, 1919), 425.

———. Review of *The Law of Civilization and Decay* by Brooks Adams. *American Historical Review*, Vol. I (April, 1896), 568–69.

Bibliography

———. Review of *The New Empire* by Brooks Adams. *Outlook*, Vol. LXXIII (January 24, 1903), 218–19.

———. Review of *The Theory of Social Revolutions* by Brooks Adams. *New York Times Book Review*, Vol. XVII (December 7, 1913), 717.

———. Review of *The Theory of Social Revolutions* by Brooks Adams. *Review of Reviews*, Vol. XLVIII (November, 1913), 635.

Boynton, H. W. Review of *The New Empire* by Brooks Adams. *Atlantic Monthly*, Vol. CXI (March, 1903), 422.

Coulborn, Runston. Review of *The Law of Civilization and Decay* by Brooks Adams. *American Historical Review*, Vol. XLIX (October, 1943), 77–78.

Day, Clive. Review of *The New Empire* by Brooks Adams. *Yale Review*, Vol. XI (February, 1903), 421–23.

Lyall, A. C. Review of *The Law of Civilization and Decay* by Brooks Adams. *Edinburgh Review*, Vol. CLXXXIII (January, 1896), 237–39.

Pierce, Donald J. Review of *The Law of Civilization and Decay* by Brooks Adams. *Political Science Quarterly*, Vol. LVIII (September, 1943), 437–38.

Richards, Edmund C. Review of *The Law of Civilization and Decay* by Brooks Adams. *New York Times Book Review* (June 13, 1943), 3.

Robbins, James J. Review of *The Law of Civilization and Decay* by Brooks Adams. *American Political Science Review*, Vol. XXXVII (August, 1943), 762–63.

Roosevelt, Theodore. Review of *The Law of Civilization and Decay* by Brooks Adams. *Forum*, Vol. LIV (October, 1943), 65.

Shotwell, James T. Review of *The New Empire* by Brooks Adams. *Political Science Quarterly*, Vol. XVIII (December, 1903), 688–93.

Stewart, John L. Review of *The Law of Civilization and Decay* by Brooks Adams. *Annals, American Academy of Political and Social Science*, Vol. VIII (July, 1896), 162–67.

Thompson, Lowell. Review of *The Law of Civilization and Decay* by Brooks Adams. *Saturday Review of Literature*, Vol. XXVI (June 19, 1943), 30.

Veblen, Thorstein. Review of *The New Empire* by Brooks Adams. *Journal of Political Economy*, Vol. XI (March, 1903), 314–15.

Wasson, D. A. Review of *The Emancipation of Massachusetts* by Brooks Adams. *Atlantic Monthly*, Vol. LIX (February, 1887), 251–57.

Wergeland, A. M. Review of *The New Empire* by Brooks Adams. *Dial*, Vol. XXXVI (January 1, 1904), 13–15.

V. SECONDARY MATERIALS: MISCELLANEOUS

1. *Books*

Adams, James Truslow. *The Adams Family*. Boston, Little, Brown & Co., 1930.

———. *The Epic of America*. Boston, Little, Brown & Co., 1931.

Ausubel, Herman. *Historians and Their Craft*. New York, Columbia University Press, 1950.

Barnes, Harry E. *The New History and the Social Studies*. New York, The Century Co., 1925.

Barraclough, Geoffrey. *History in a Changing World*. Norman, University of Oklahoma Press, 1955.

Bellot, H. Hale. *American History and American Historians*. Norman, University of Oklahoma Press, 1952.

Blackmur, Richard P. *The Lion and the Honeycomb: Essays in Solicitude and Critique*. New York, Harcourt, Brace & Co., 1955.

Breasted, James H. *A History of Egypt*. New York, Macmillan Co., 1942.

Brogan, D. W. *American Themes*. New York, Harper and Brothers, 1947.

Brooks, Van Wyck. *New England: Indian Summer, 1865–1915*. New York, E. P. Dutton & Co., 1940.

Burns, Edward M. *The American Idea of Mission*. New Brunswick, Rutgers University Press, 1957.

Bury, J. B. *The Idea of Progress*. With an introduction by Charles A. Beard. New York, Dover Publications, Inc., 1955.

Bibliography

Cargill, Oscar. *Intellectual America: Ideas on the March*. New York, Macmillan Co., 1941.

Carpenter, Frederic I. *American Literature and the Dream*. New York, Philosophical Library, 1955.

Commager, Henry S. *The American Mind*. New Haven, Yale University Press, 1950.

Curti, Merle E. *The Growth of American Thought*. New York, Harper and Brothers, 1943.

Elliott, W. Y. *The Pragmatic Revolt in Politics*. New York, Macmillan Co., 1928.

Gabriel, Ralph H. *The Course of American Democratic Thought*. New York, Ronald Press Co., 1940.

Giddings, F. L. *Studies in the Theory of Human Society*. New York, Macmillan Co., 1922.

Goldman, Eric F., ed. *Historiography and Urbanization: Essays in American History in Honor of W. Stull Holt*. Baltimore, Johns Hopkins Press, 1941.

Hays, Samuel P. *The Response to Industrialism, 1885–1914*. Chicago, University of Chicago Press, 1957.

Hicks, Granville. *The Great Tradition*. New York, Macmillan Co., 1933.

Hofstadter, Richard. *The American Political Tradition and the Men Who Made It*. New York, Alfred A. Knopf., Inc., 1948.

———. *Social Darwinism in American Thought*. Philadelphia, University of Pennsylvania Press, 1945.

Kazin, Alfred M. *On Native Grounds*. Vintage Edition. New York, Alfred A. Knopf, Inc., 1956.

Kraus, Michael F. *The Writing of American History*. Norman, University of Oklahoma Press, 1953.

Lewisohn, Ludwig. *Expression in America*. New York, Harper and Brothers, 1932.

May, Henry F. *The End of American Innocence*. New York, Alfred A. Knopf, Inc., 1959.

Morris, Lloyd. *Postscript to Yesterday*. New York, Random House, 1947.

Parrington, V. L. *Main Currents in American Thought*. New York, Harcourt, Brace & Co., 1927.

Persons, Stow. *American Minds*. New York, Henry Holt and
Co., 1958.
Saveth, Edward N. *American Historians and European Immigrants,
1875–1925*. New York, Columbia University Press, 1948.
Smith, Joe Patterson. "Francis Parkman," in William T. Hutchin-
son (ed.), *The Marcus Jernegan Essays in American Historiog-
raphy*. Chicago, University of Chicago Press. 1937.
Spengler, Oswald. *The Decline of the West*. 2 vols. New York,
Alfred A. Knopf., Inc., 1929.
Stovall, Floyd. *American Idealism*. Norman, University of Okla-
homa Press, 1943.
Strout, Cushing. *The Pragmatic Revolt in American History: Carl
Becker and Charles Beard*. New Haven, Yale University Press,
1958.
Toynbee, Arnold J. *A Study of History*. 10 vols. London, Oxford
University Press, 1934–54.
Wolfe, Don M. *The Image of Man in America*. Dallas, Southern
Methodist University Press, 1957.

2. *Articles*

Beard, Charles A. "Historians at Work: Brooks and Henry Adams,"
Atlantic Monthly, Vol. CLXXI (April, 1943), 87–98.
———. "Written History as an Act of Faith," *American Historical
Review*, Vol. XXXIX (January, 1934), 219–29.
Cheyney, Edward P. "Law in History," *American Historical Re-
view*, Vol. XXIX (January, 1924), 231–48.
Destler, Chester M. "Some Observations on Contemporary His-
torical Theory," *American Historical Review*, Vol. CV (April,
1950), 503–29.
Langer, William D. "The Next Assignment," *American Historical
Review*, Vol. LXIII (January, 1958), 283–304.
Sherman, Stuart P. "Evolution in the Adams Family," *Nation*, Vol.
CX (April 10, 1920), 473–77.
Taylor, Henry Osborn. "A Layman's View of History," *American
Historical Review*, Vol. XXXIII (January, 1928), 247–56.

Index

Aaron, Daniel: 194
Abélard, Peter: 61, 64
Adams, Brooks: concern for America, 5–6; rejection of family traditions, 11–12; sense of alienation, 20; prediction of American fate, 22; Comte's influence upon, 28; concern for future, 33–34; attitude on cause and effect, 67; on the nature of history, 68–71; on tools for historians, 71–72; on methodological vices of historians, 72–76; on religious faith, 76–78; on age of imagination, 79–80; on disintegration of religious age, 80–81; on wealth, 82–83; on transition to capitalism, 83–84; on judicial systems, 84; on economic determinism, 85–86; on Darwinism, 87–93; compared to Henry, 95, 97, 98, 99, 100, 101, 150–56; criticism of, 96; explanation of law of civilization, 127–28; and age of religion, 129–30; and age of competition, 130–31; and cycles of civilization, 132–34; on applying law, 135–36; on importance of trade routes, 136–37; and the decline of Rome, 138–39; and the rise of England, 139–40; on failures of Spain and France, 140–41; on election of 1828, 141; on Japanese expansion, 141–42; and American institutions, 142–44; criticism of the law of, 144–49; and dream tradition, 157, 160; and American promise, 164–65; and national feeling, 165; on the South 167; on judicial defects, 168–69; on collectivism, 170; on American leadership, 174–75; and the Civil War, 178–79; and the Spanish-American War, 181–83; and the new dream, 184–85; on universality of history, 187; and scientific history, 188–89; final evaluation of, 191–94

Index